SPIRITLINKING LEADERSHIP

Working through Resistance to Organizational Change

DONNA J. MARKHAM

PAULIST PRESS

New York / Mahwah, N.J.

Cover design by PAZ Design Group

Author photo by Jac Jacobson Photographics Inc.

Interior design by Millennium Wordpress

LIBRARY OF CONGRESS CATALOGING-IN-PUBLICATION DATA

Markham, Donna J.
    Spiritlinking leadership : working through resistance to achieve organizational change / Donna J. Markham.
        p.   cm.
    Includes bibliographical references.
    ISBN 0-8091-3840-9 (alk. paper)
    1. Organizational change. 2. Leadership. I. Title.
HD58.8.M26526   1998
658.4′063–dc21   98–49088
                                                                                                                        CIP

Published by Paulist Press
997 Macarthur Boulevard
Mahwah, New Jersey 07430

www.paulistpress.com

Printed and bound in the
United States of America

CONTENTS

ACKNOWLEDGMENTS   vi

FOREWORD by Theo Theodosiou   viii

PREFACE   xi

1. SPIRITLINKING...AN INTRODUCTION   1

    Spiritlinking: The Need   2
    The Challenge   4
    Bridging Disunity and Promoting Community   4
    Deepening a Sense of Meaning   10
    The Skills   11
    Managing Vision   11
    Creating Synergy through Sustaining Creative Conflict   13
    Working through Grief and Resistance   16
    Your Turn....   18

2. WORKING THROUGH RESISTANCE   23

    Static vs. Agitated Resistance   27
    Manifestations of Resistance   29
    Signs and Symptoms of Resistance at Work   40
    Process of Working through Resistance   41
    Your Turn....   46

3. SPIRITLINKING, TRUTH TELLING AND
    INCREASING THE PAIN   50

    Truth Telling and Disequilibrium   52
    Cave Keeping   55
    Attempting to Keep Balance   59
    Exploring a Spiritlinking Alternative   62
    Wonder in the Midst of the Mess   64
    Your Turn....   66

4. LEADING FOR THE COMMON GOOD   67

    Perspectives on the Common Good   73
    Becoming Comfortable with and Adept at Handling Conflict 76
    Guarding against Groupthink   80
    Promoting Efficacious Communal Action   84
    Working through Resistance—a Case Example   85
    Your Turn....   89

5. FOSTERING COMMUNITY, INTERPRETING METAPHORS   92

    Listening to the Metaphor   93
    The Corporate Community as Metaphor   95
    Resistance to Collaboration   98
    The Collaborative Work Community   104
    The Promise of a Corporate Community Realized   106
    Your Turn....   109

6. PROVIDING HEALTHY LEADERSHIP   113

    The Unrecovering Addict   115
    The Narcissist as Leader   117
    The "As-If" Leader in the Empty Suit   120
    The Talking Head as Leader   122

The Spiritlinking Leader   123
Staying Healthy   125
Your Turn....   126

7. PUTTING IT ALL TOGETHER   130

Linking   131
Grounding   133
Illuminating Energy   136
You've Got the Last Word....   138

NOTES   140

RECOMMENDED READING   141

DEDICATION

for Dad

ACKNOWLEDGMENTS

The encouragement to write this book came from persons from many walks of life and from many different parts of the world. Business executives, health care professionals, educators and church leaders; artists, poets, shamans and refugees; those who lead multinational corporations and those who walk with the disenfranchised, have all provided me with courage and inspiration. I am especially grateful to the Adrian Dominicans, colleagues from Worldbridges, the Windstar Foundation, the Southdown Institute and the CHW Health System. The process itself has truly invigorated my spirit as ideas have been shaped and refined through wonderful conversations and the love and support of many dear friends.

THE AUTHOR

Donna J. Markham is the President and CEO of the Southdown Institute in Ontario, Canada. She has held a number of leadership positions in the health care field and has served on boards of directors for not-for-profit organizations and corporations in the fields of education, health care and social service. Additionally, she has served in leadership roles within the Adrian Dominican Congregation and the Leadership Conference of Women Religious in the United States. Dr. Markham obtained a doctorate in clinical psychology from the University of Detroit. She has lectured widely on topics pertaining to organization transformation, resistance to change and community building.

AUTHOR OF THE FOREWORD

Theo M. Theodosiou is a Partner with Ernst & Young, LLP. He leads Ernst & Young's change management services for the health care industry. Mr. Theodosiou has consulted for ten years, providing services to clients on a national basis. His business experiences span three continents and several industries. He has served on the faculty of ACHE, teaching courses on successfully implementing Total Quality Management (TQM) in health care and has taught conflict resolution at Northwestern University. He has been a frequent speaker for local and national organizations and boards of directors. He holds a B.B.A. in business administration from Texas A&M University and an M.S. in organizational behavior from Northwestern University. He has supported many executive leading their organizations through transformation.

FOREWORD

The works of many authors have drawn a distinction between *management* and *leadership*. Some of this literature has reduced *leadership* to glorified management: the ability to get things done in an organization. Conversely, some authors have elevated *leadership* to a near divine status, proposing that charismatic and visionary leadership is an absolute requirement for organizational success. According to the latter view, the organizational sun rises and sets through leadership alone. Fortunately, James Collins and Jerry Porras, in their pioneering work, *Built to Last*, challenge this myth. In fact, their research reveals that a charismatic, visionary leader can prove detrimental to an organization's long-term prospects. Experienced executives quickly recognize the risks posed by charismatic leaders who dominate an organization, thereby overwhelming and limiting the contributions of others.

Stephen Covey's work in the area of effective organizational leadership provides useful insights. He proposes that, on its journey, an organization is often in need of a vision and a compass (*leadership*) and less in need of a road map (*management*). This vision and compass, however, are only as meaningful as the willingness of the entire organization to accept the vision and commit its energies to completing the journey. What, then, is the appropriate role of leadership in organizational life? Is there a balance between the "pedestrian" and "divine" views of it?

In this volume Donna Markham presents a thoughtful revisiting of the concept of leadership. She does this at a different level of processing. Her work goes beyond the world of the visible and known. She wonders into the world of the intangible, of magic. Magical phenomena involve forces with a profound effect on us, those that we are at a loss to explain: faith, falling in love, parenthood. This volume adds *leadership* to that menu.

It has been suggested that we know of the presence of wind not because we can see it, but because we experience its effect: a weeping willow swaying, the sails of a ship swelling, the feeling of a summer breeze. Donna Markham views leadership in this vein. What is it that leaders do that allows the visible effects of community? They work in the white space between the lives of those around them. They link spirits and allow for the wonders that only a community of spirits can accomplish.

Actually, it is through the magic of parenthood that I was introduced to the fundamental idea that each of us is created unique. I have watched my daughter and son, Clare and Michael, now twelve and eleven, grow. Parents all over the world can testify to a certain quality siblings have: inevitably linked, uniquely different. Clare, when a second-grader, brought home from school an artifact. It was a picture of herself against a background of a snowflake and the caption: "I am as special as a snowflake. One of a kind."

Clare was born to us with Down's syndrome and for the first time, reading the snowflake caption, I was able to put her special needs and distinctive features into a new context. Clare is unique and special—not because she was born with special needs, but because every child, every human is unique and special. We all are delicate and vulnerable. In this context, the words of Nelson Mandela resonate with meaning: "We were born to manifest the glory of God within us. It's not just in some of us; it's in everyone." It is in Clare and Michael and in you and in me.

Immense is the burden of parenthood: the need to provide structure to the child without suffocating and damaging that snowflake. In the world of grown-ups, we are each as unique and vulnerable as the children we used to be. Spiritlinking leaders recognize the responsibility vested in them to balance individuality and community. They must possess not only the ability to connect snowflakes without touching them but also the ability to invite each of us to connect with others. Karl E. Weick's concept of "loosely coupled" organizations and the variations of that idea that have followed are premised on our uniqueness as individuals and our ability to reinvent not ourselves but the way we work with each other.

The potential for the application of spiritlinking ideas is tremendous. This truth was recently brought home to me in a simple though telling way during

the process of my assisting an organization to build a new business. This new business includes a call center operation with about five hundred people located under a single roof. With the new building almost complete, we are in the process of finalizing the arrangements for the move. In conjunction with these plans, the employees were invited to select which one out of three chairs they would like to be assigned. I was amazed at the reaction of the staff as they answered this invitation. Enthusiastically, they lined up to choose the chair they preferred. I couldn't help but reflect on how limiting our approach to employees has been if such enthusiasm was generated over so limited a freedom.

This book returns us to the possibilities of rediscovering the balance and boundaries between individuality and community. Spiritlinking leaders, most assuredly, can pave the way.

—Theo M. Theodosiou
Partner
Ernst & Young, LLP

PREFACE

Aliyeh is a thirty-three-year-old refugee who came to speak with me because of terrible nightmares she was having about her escape from Eritrea, Africa. When I met her, although she spoke in a soft whisper, her emaciated frame screamed of the torture she had experienced. She had walked for forty-seven days across the desert into Sudan. When her feet became too infected for her to walk any farther, she and three companions hid among some boulders to avoid the bombs and mortar fire. Hidden in the rocks, she closed her eyes tightly because, as she says now so simply, "I did not want to see me die." She told her friends to go on without her because her pained pace would place them at risk. But her companions would not leave her there to die alone. They carried her on their backs until they reached Sudan.

Aliyeh left her country, her successful work as a nurse, her family and her land, and she ran for her life. She knew that to stay where she was, in familiar surroundings with well-learned patterns of living and behaving, would mean certain death.

Like Aliyeh, perhaps in a no-less-dramatic way, those of us in leadership today are faced with the abandonment of everything that once felt secure, and, like Aliyeh, we cannot go it alone. We are faced with the grieving that comes in the long walk in the desert when we have left behind everything familiar and enter into uncertainty. Excellent leaders know that what seemed secure yesterday is dangerously inadequate to meet the needs of today. To the extent that this reality is denied and old patterns of conducting business are retained simply because they once worked well, our organizations will face extinction.

Some leaders are focused on and committed to ending this death play as it taunts our institutions and corporations; others are deeply committed to stopping it at national and international levels as leaders who work to end war and stop human slaughter; others work toward the process of global transformation in their commitment to reversing the loss of our topsoil, our forests and our wildlife; still others face the need for transformation in the ravaged look on the human face. Regardless of our specific point of entry, we enter this time together as leaders—to link hearts and spirits—to put an end to destructive forces that threaten global and social well-being.

We are here now, we are conscious, and by the accident of our citizenship and the power of our education we are obligated to lead. We hold the power and the energy to link spirits for the future of the good we hold in common. We dare not close our eyes to avoid watching us and all around us die.

The purpose of this book is to focus on those tasks necessary for leaders committed to organizational transformation—spiritlinking leaders—those creative, feisty and fearless folk who will dare to traverse the terrain of predictable resistances in order to lead into the new. Throughout the book, the terms *leader, leadership team* and *management team* are used. Because spiritlinking rightfully applies to the mandate of all who bear any responsibility in fashioning or helping to facilitate the direction of an organization or institution, a department or a work group, no attempt has been made to make distinctions in the definitions of these terms. The shared obligation of all who serve in any leadership capacity is the engagement in interdependent, cooperative and dynamic action on behalf of the good that is held in common. Such creative engagement calls for a spirit of courageous imagination in considering what might be, along with a spirit of humble relinquishment in letting go of what has been. Thus, this is a book for those who dare to face the grieving that is part of an arduous yet exciting trek. It is a book for those who are curious, value-driven, compassionate and bold enough to take some delight in chaos and in the lack of absolute certitude. Perhaps more pointedly, this is a book for those leaders who, in the solitude of their more reflective moments, find their spirits nourished in the sacred exploration of those unsettling questions about the meaning of their work in this world.

The second part of each chapter affords the reader opportunities for applying concepts to their current organizational realities. In "Your Turn," practical information and questions are provided for discussion at board retreats, planning retreats, management team meetings or simply for personal reflection.

Most of all, this is a book inviting the reader to engage with others in working with the human dynamic of resistance to transformative change as we press on together to create a global community committed to promoting a more compassionate and safer life for future generations.

Chapter 1

SPIRITLINKING...AN INTRODUCTION

Recently, during a last-minute dash to the airport, I was trying desperately to retain some semblance of poise as my anxiety escalated to threshold levels. I was anticipating meeting an angry group of health care administrators who, I imagined, would be preparing for the kill when I arrived. They had been informed that their board of directors had mandated "right-sizing," and that a potential merger with another facility was in the offing. I had been sent to facilitate the expression of their feelings and to begin the painful process of individuals' termination.

I caught the plane to the coast and, after several anxious hours, arrived at my destination. Soon I was engaged in a tense series of sessions on "conflict management" (a wonderful euphemism to characterize that day). After spending the next day at the ocean to recuperate from the fray, I flew home.

Upon arriving at the airport, I reached for my keys—not there. I rifled through the wadded potpourri of old direction notes, phone messages and to-do lists in my purse. The keys were definitely not there. Surreptitiously I whispered to the van driver that I didn't have my keys. Next came the driver's embarrassingly loud public announcement, overheard by all the other business people jammed into the parking-lot shuttle: "No problem, lady—lost keys? I'll just take you last."

When I was finally driven to my car, I saw there were no keys inside. I proceeded to the main office. There, on a large piece of tagboard, in the company of dozens of other lost keys, was my key ring, wrapped in a crumpled piece of paper with a rubber band around it. I opened the note and read, "Keys locked in car. Motor running."

Spiritlinking: The Need

This incident epitomizes what it is like to be in leadership today—running fast...covering lots of territory...trying to keep up the pace...spotting troubles ahead... fighting off loss of control...trying to stay calm. Leaders are not always equipped with the right keys, but the motor keeps running nonetheless. Whorls of complexity, unpredictability, disequilibrium and rapid reconfiguration, compounded by financial uncertainty and fuzzy vision, coalesce to heighten anxiety. Yesterday's strategies are not only woefully obsolete but also downright inane. Where are the right keys?

In these times of ambiguity and extraordinary complexity, when anxiety is high and chaos abounds, how do leaders promote human worth, dignity and creativity? How do they contribute to the collective soul search for meaning in the workplace? The key to addressing the challenges that face those who are, or who will become, our excellent leaders is **spiritlinking**—*the deliberate and untiring act of working through resistance to organizational transformation by building the circle of friends, fostering networks of human compassion and interweaving teams of relationships through which new ideas are born and new* *ways of responding to the mission take form and find expression.* Spiritlinking describes the basis for actualizing the living covenant between the human community and the world matrix in which humankind lives and works. It capitalizes on the organizational energy that is released as resistance to change is persistently addressed. Without spiritlinking activity, both global and organizational survival are in jeopardy. Spiritlinking is foundational to profound systemic change and describes behaviors vital to provoking the upheaval of the status quo for the sake of the organizational mission. It encompasses the challenge to leaders to bridge disunity through fostering community and instilling a deepened sense of meaning in work. At the same time, it demands that leaders possess the skill to manage vision and conflict, as these "spiritlinks" contain enormous reservoirs of energy to be released for global viability. As mission relates to life purpose, spiritlinking speaks to enlivening and invigorating that purpose for the sake of future generations. At its essence, spiritlinking entails the steady working through of all the manifestations of resistance to transformation that human beings and organizations unconsciously create to defend themselves from the unknown. The word itself conveys the sense of hope and excitement that is embedded in today's confusion. It speaks to the inner desire to establish connection with others at the "heart of the matter," and it portends a sense of the energy and life that are freed when that bonding of the heart and spirit is made. It has a lot to do with courage, chaos, frustration tolerance and love, and it has a lot to do with what is entailed in being an excellent leader.

The birth of the term *spiritlinking* brought to mind a lovely insight from Maya Angelou: "Spirit is an invisible force made visible in all life....Spirit is one and is everywhere present...it is this belief which allows me to venture into the unknown and even the unknowable...."[1] We cannot go it alone, nor can we simply engage in practices that merely network our businesses and institutions and invite us to perfunctory interaction. We are entreated to relate at the level of the life-stuff that beckons us to respect, reverence, creativity and energy. If we are to head into the future with stamina and the common wisdom to venture into what is yet to be discovered or created, it is necessary to link our spirits.

The Challenge

BRIDGING DISUNITY AND PROMOTING COMMUNITY

Spiritlinking is directed toward networking, community forming and coalition building across chasms of ideological differences. It is a daring, disruptive, counter-cultural and revolutionary activity that flies in the face of popular trends toward individualism, separatism and organizational self-sufficiency and autonomy—all subtle resistances to the process of transformation. It stands in direct contradiction to millenarian thinking that says: "Humanity is progressing very nicely the way it always has; business is fine. We're only on this earth temporarily and, in fact, the world is probably coming to an end, and we'll all go on to a better life anyhow, so let's not upset the way things have always been done. Our concern should be with our corporate economic profitability and personal well-being, and we shouldn't waste time in risky acts of creative transformation and envisioning the new. Let's just keep things the way they've always been, enjoy life today and not worry about the next generation."

Harvard zoologist Edward O. Wilson has been quoted upon occasion as saying that this logic is an example of

SPIRITLINKING:

The Deliberate and

Untiring Act of

Working through Resistance

to Organizational Transformation

by Building the Circle of Friends,

Fostering Networks of

Human Compassion

and Interweaving Teams of Relationships

through Which New Ideas Are Born

and New Ways of Responding

to the Mission

Take Form and Find Expression

living in a high-tech world with Paleolithic brains. An organization that continues with such an isolationist mentality is moribund. Its spirit is being stifled under waves of narrowly defined tradition. It may very well be that the social sin of the next century—the choice of death over life—will be that of resistance to community. History is replete with the deadly consequences of righteous separatism and arrogant self-interest that have led inevitably to downfall and destruction. The Roman Empire, the Third Reich and colonial expansionism are classic examples of political movements contrary to the formation of a respectful interdependent world community, while global deforestation and the destruction of rain forests are sobering contemporary examples of rampant violation of the ecological interdependence (or communion, if you will) of living organisms.

It is through concerted efforts to build community in every segment of society that global healing is promoted and the likelihood of destruction is diminished. The power of corporations and institutions toward the accomplishment of this effort cannot be underestimated. The development of organizational communities catalyzes global spiritlinking and represents the best efforts of our most talented, dedicated and mission-driven leaders.

"Conflict and resistance become means of solidifying rather than dividing people."

Organizational communities are places where the wonder and surprises that emerge from chaos and confusion can be explored, where open communication, confrontation, conflict and compassion explode and coalesce to create the new paradigm. Conflict and resistance become means of solidifying rather than dividing people. Oddly, peaceful adherence to the current culture is far more likely to erode communitarian effectiveness, whereas—albeit, somewhat counterintuitively—challenge and well-managed conflict actually promote cohesion in the long term. To foster spiritlinking is to transcend the pull of

CHALLENGES FOR SPIRITLINKING

• Bridge Disunity

• Promote Community

• Deepen Sense of Meaning

• Heighten Creativity

Across Chasms of Differences

individualism through the formation of networked, communal teams that grapple with resistance and contend nonviolently with challenge and conflict. At the global level, spiritlinking efforts establish meeting places of minds and hearts where conflicting forces and positions seek common ground. Thus, by its very nature, spiritlinking fosters institutional upset as heightened communication and divergent, and often conflictual, opinions predictably result in periodic feelings of chaos as resistances to change are discovered and confronted. It is under the shroud of such a paradox, in the midst of the confusion and stress of conflictual dialogue, that the potential for deadly conflict is mitigated.

Spiritlinking defies arrogance. One way to measure organizational health is the extent to which differences of opinion and boundary-crossing interaction occur within the work community. This viewpoint begs the question: Are members of the organization encouraged to enter into dialogue with those whose roles are perceived to be "subordinate" to or "superior" to their own? When communication is limited or controlled by outmoded, rigidified authority structures that prohibit human beings from interacting, spiritlinking is aborted in the silence. Community is stagnated.

Spiritlinking leaders are, themselves, not structured into rigid patterns of relating nor do they bind their coworkers by prosaic organizational charts. They do not define their relationships with employees by their authority positions. These leaders are profoundly aware that each person in the organization is a unit of creativity and energy[2] with something valuable to contribute to the wisdom of the whole. The organization is, in itself, a living organism—vibrant and purposeful—capitalizing on the connective interplay of all who comprise it. Spiritlinking leaders trust that it is precisely because of employees' collective inner wonder and, their inquisitiveness and spirit that new ways of doing business will develop and massive energy will be freed to serve the mission of the organization.

Today's leadership is about unifying and linking persons for the sake of the future quality and dignity of life for all living beings. Good leaders promote the unity of their organizations by believing in the worth and value of each person. There is no place in leadership today for individuals who are locked into attitudes of self-importance and the narcissism that purports that lines of communication are restricted to top management. Organizations run by such people will not survive because these leaders limit the staff's spirit, disengage its energy and strand themselves on self-protected turf. They entrench themselves in resistance. While authority and leadership are essential to the functioning of any group, rigidly structured hierarchic authority lines that promote stability and order will doom any group. This will happen because synergistic, highly creative imagining and decision making are thwarted by limited communication, limited access to information and a lack of openness and respect for the contributions of each and every member. Consequently, the group suffers from loss of morale and attrition of personnel. Arrogant self-sufficiency has taken its toll.

In contrast, the spiritlinking leader asks, to what extent do persons within the organization feel comfortable and enriched by interacting with those who are serving different functions? For example, does a maintenance person or housekeeper feel welcomed in conversation with senior management? Is the CEO's office off-limits to anyone other than top-level staff? The bottom line becomes whether persons in the organization feel valued and respected. Bridge building happens across social strata and organizational titles. When we reverence the fact that each person in the organization—female or male, conservative or liberal, formally educated or educated by life, dominant race or visible minority—has something enormously important to contribute to the collective wisdom of the whole, then the organization stands poised for massive transformative communal energy to be released. Line communication has been replaced by networked, matrix interaction that deliberately encourages information sharing, and interaction across disciplines and, perhaps most problematically, invites differences of opinion. Admittedly, there is an enormous challenge in organizational community building. Persons may work longer hours because less time is spent alone attending to executive tasks that still need attention. Work time is filled with far more interaction and is characterized more by interruption than by single-minded task accomplishment. Nonetheless, work time becomes a source of personal energy rather than a forum for promoting exhaustion, and the vibrancy of corporate life invigorates the very environment to which it is connected.

DEEPENING A SENSE OF MEANING

When employment in an organization is solely a means of acquiring an income, when work is no more than a job and persons no more than enfleshed robots who fill perfunctory functions designed to address immediate needs, meaninglessness begins to gnaw at the core of the group. Energy and creativity are drained as employees take less initiative and fewer risks. A clear understanding and commitment to an overwhelming mission affords meaning to an organization. What is the life purpose of the organization? How does that purpose better the world matrix? How are values enfleshed in the workplace? Is there any corporate consciousness of the needs of the disenfranchised? How does compassion find a face in the organization? Spiritlinking leaders inspire others to reflect upon the larger vision where work holds the promise of expressing those values destined to improve the quality of life in a sustainable global community.

"The absence of reflective spirit in a group results in a depletion of commitment."

The absence of reflective spirit in a group results in a depletion of commitment. Leaders who call upon their organizations to probe the questions "Why are we doing this?" and "How are we making a difference in our world?" invite persons into an accounting of the corporate conscience that inspires pride and meaning in the work that is undertaken. Such a process of reflection counters the pull toward emptiness and meaningless that taunts an era of massive change and serves to balance anxiety-driven activism.

On a practical level, when leaders face the challenge of raising the *meaning questions* in the board room as well as in the workplace, they inspire others, through their own mentoring, to evaluate corporate decisions and actions consistently in light of serious reflection upon fidelity to their mission.

The Skills

Effective leadership is about liberation, about loving, about listening, about telling the truth and taking risks, about solidifying the circle of friends for the sake of the mission. Spiritlinking leaders are mentors committed to open communication, to serving and to making sure conflict is managed well. Every human organization responds in an unconscious and intricately exquisite way either to the health or to the pathology of its leader. As groups reflect the pathology of their leaders, it becomes all the more crucial that leaders themselves do not drift into dysfunctional relational or behavioral patterns. Disturbed, conflicted leaders breed sick, paranoiac organizations that are mired in survival and maintenance agendas. Leaders who are healthy will inspire courage and integrity as their organizations risk to embody a mission-driven mandate to enter into the transformative process. These effective leaders focus on the future, on the realization of the mission—not on maintaining things the way they are or on reinforcing the parameters of resistance to change. Maintenance leaders burn out quickly and their organizations flounder. The ability to manage vision, create synergy, sustain creative conflict and work through grief and resistance is clearly dependent on a psychologically healthy, secure and flexible ego able to subordinate personal needs to the needs of the organization, as this is appropriate.

MANAGING VISION

Some define the role of the leader as the individual who holds within his or her imagination some clear destination where the organization should arrive within a given amount of time. This leader should possess the ability to inspire enough enthusiasm within the group to enable it to move forward. Others see the leader as a grand facilitator of input that cocreates a vision statement for a preferred future. The delusion is this: The clearer the vision statement—the better the odds of accomplishing it!

These styles are not only impossible but may be quite undesirable today. There can be no fixed vision, no preferred state in this time of cataclysmic change. While it may be comforting to bind organizational anxiety through processes designed to articulate a clear vision, it may be more honest to admit that there can be only visionary direction. Vision, at best, is fuzzy business.

Recall going to work on a morning when the trees and the streets were shrouded in fog. There is a strange, eerie beauty in that experience but also an edgy discomfort because it is not clear what lies ahead. Something is in the distance, but its shape and nature are not yet clear. The road ahead is just visible enough to allow continuing on. Like fog, vision swirls into every corner of an organization as light and energy are reflected in and around everyone and everything that is encompassed by it. Boundaries and outlines are neither clear nor precise. Destinations are impossible to see with certainty, but there is a sense of going in the right direction. Visions, foggy though they may be, surround and are absorbed by each member of the organization and each workspace. Like bone-permeating fog, visions are transmitted and diffused, modified and reshaped as they link all parts of the organization along the journey toward transformation. They seep into the very fiber of the organization as they maintain some kind of mysterious motion hovering over and permeating remote areas into which they can expand. Spiritlinking happens in the fog as it unfolds new images and insight at each milepost along the way.

Spiritlinking leaders learn to navigate in the fog. They have a sense of direction but no clear or absolute vision of the destination. They are confident in the direction because they are passionately committed to the mission of the organization. Mission gives direction to vision. These leaders generate courage and the belief that as long as persons are connected and unified in single-minded commitment to the mission that is yet hazy and amorphous, the swirling and fuzzy vista ahead is filled with possibility and potential. For this to happen, leaders must eliminate the impact of fear on those who work with them. Fear of making mistakes, fear of doing something differently, fear of getting lost for a while, fear of conflict—all these fears serve to entice people to return to the certainty of safe but overworn roads. At the same time, spiritlinking leaders have a strong capacity to tolerate ambiguity because changing pace and direction may be necessary as they unify the organization that is moving forward into the haze.

"Mission gives direction to vision."

While it would be foolhardy for companies to abandon processes of articulating their missions, visions and goals and the strategies necessary to achieve them, it would be equally imprudent to cast visions in stone. Tolerance for ambiguity, the capacity to live in the absence of certainty, is a sign of mental health not only in individuals but in corporations as well. To resort to rigid compartmentalization in organizational planning processes is to endorse an anachronistic, reductionistic, hierarchical approach to the world.

CREATING SYNERGY THROUGH SUSTAINING CREATIVE CONFLICT

The promotion and management of conflict are benchmarks of a healthy organization; yet conflict is something from which most persons tend to back away.

SKILLS FOR SPIRITLINKING

· Manage Vision

· Create Synergy

· Sustain Conflict

· Work through Grief and Resistance

by Continually Dealing with
Organizational Resistance

Left unattended, conflict becomes one of the most powerful resistances to change. A stereotypical understanding of conflict—that it is to be squelched or avoided at all costs—blocks the possibility of synergistic, highly creative solutions to the complex problems that face organizations these days. It is no longer sufficient to speak about conflict resolution but, rather, how can healthy conflict be promoted and managed?

Conflict resolution assumed that most, if not all, conflictual situations were problematic and destructive and that what was needed was a methodology to restore peace. This led many groups to an overreliance on a primitive understanding of the use of consensus and often put closure on problem solving before the best solutions were identified. Early conceptualizations of consensus suggested that consensus was reached when everyone could "live with" the decision. Moreover, it frequently led to a watered-down conclusion that held little passion for implementation. This, in turn, left leaders puzzled by the lack of ownership and the inability to actualize decisions that had been made precisely because persons settled on a resolution that everyone could live with but that held little excitement or passion for anyone.

Debate and conflict are uncomfortable, messy and demanding, but spiritlinking happens in the midst of the mess when colleagues find their voices and speak their truth. When peers agree to stay in creative tension in the service of the good that is held in common, they touch upon the wondrous possibility of participating in the breaking in of the spirit when truth cracks through staid patterns of thinking and transforming vision takes new form and expression. They just may experience synergy: *the energy-laden, unexpected accord—or communion— that emerges in a group so that momentum can be channeled toward the good that is held in common.*

Spiritlinking leaders commit to conflict that does no harm, conflict that serves to link spirits and free the best of the organizational creativity that is, above all else, contained in profound respect for and right relationship with others. That being said, it would be simplistic to think that all conflict is positive. Obviously, conflict that results in exploitation, destruction, diminishment or devaluation must be squelched at all costs. The spiritlinking leader acts on the side of life and the releasing of energy for the accomplishment of the organizational mission. Thus, any manifestation of conflict that is disrespectful of life must be halted because, rather than leading toward synergy, it results in personal and organizational fragmentation.

An erroneous yet quite pervasive cultural and emotional equation prevails that equates all experiences of conflict with destruction. Excellent leaders refute this equation as they take the fear out of healthy conflict; that is, they promote respectful debate and encourage

"The spiritlinking leader acts on the side of life and the releasing of energy for the accomplishments of the organizational mission."

differences of perspective and insight. While aware that there are those times of threatened organizational polarization when consensus strategies are appropriate, they shy away from overreliance on a consensual posture that offers resolutions that everyone can simply tolerate. Spiritlinking leaders set the stage for the surprise of synergy.

WORKING THROUGH GRIEF AND RESISTANCE

Spiritlinking is upsetting and unsettling because it touches into the heart of an organization's existence. That is, out of the confusion and the chaos of these times, it is called to let go and to believe in the terrifying awe of new life. Wonder beckons the vibrant organization to believe beyond fear, to leap beyond doubt and to risk beyond its dreams. An agitated resistance to such paradigmatic revolution is an expected consequence for an organization that will be effective and relevant in the times ahead. Many forward-thinking leaders, however, have failed to recognize the power of unattended grieving as former ways of going about business have necessarily been relinquished. Internalized grief is frequently at the root of low morale and palpable corporate malaise. While the need to ritualize endings has frequently been addressed, the grip of unresolved grief will continue to exert its resistant force on an organization that has not fully worked through such important affect. In the avoidance of engaging in the process of working through this corporate affect, grief becomes a formidable foundation for depressive forms of unconscious resistance destined to become increasingly destructive if they continue to be ignored.

While many leaders acknowledge the importance of working through resistance to corporate transformation, it has been difficult to know precisely how to do this. Therefore, many organizations have lost valuable time as the transformative process has been held at bay by various unsuspected resistant strategies. "Working through" is used to describe the *management* of resistance rather than the *resolution* of it. This is an important distinction because resistance will never go away. It persists in the life of any living group that faces change. The ability to work through resistance suggests that it is a constant reality that can be engaged to operate to the good of the organization. The effective leader works through resistance by: (1) identifying the mode of the resistant behavior; (2) engaging the organization in exploring the motive behind the manifestation of resistance at this particular moment; (3) exploring the implications that the resistant behavior holds for the future life of the organization if it is left unaddressed; and (4) determining the action the organization is willing to take to move beyond the resistance. This critical skill for the spiritlinking leader will be discussed more fully in the next chapter. Resistance works through the organization like a three-dimensional spiral that continues its circling, intensifying its presence the closer the organization comes to the heart of its transformation. While it can obstruct the process of corporate transformation, it also serves an adaptive function as it ensures against an organization that is changing simply for the sake of change. A complex mechanism, the benefits of resistance are made available to a company when the unconscious dynamics are raised to awareness by the discerning leader. To that end, at each point of the appearance of potentially resistant behaviors, leaders engage the group in reflective discussion that addresses the four components of the process of *working through resistance* (i.e., the mode, the motive, the meaning and the action to be taken). In this way, the energy that could be directed toward organizational paralysis is directed instead toward freeing the organization to take yet another step in its transformative process.

The wisdom emerging from across diverse disciplines purports that the new paradigm will arise from the fomenting chaos that pervades much of human experience today. In the midst of uncertainty and confusion, chaos theorists assure, there is an inherently exquisite and complex order that yet remains hidden. As chaos increases, a self-organizing principle takes over, until one day the new paradigm will become surprisingly apparent. Spiritlinking leaders are desperately needed in the midst of this maelstrom to announce the promise that there is at work in our world and within our organizations a life-generating energy straining to author a new global communion.

Your Turn....

- Bridging disharmony and promoting the unity of the entire organization is a principal mandate for spiritlinking leadership. To do this, the astute leadership team must be able to identify those areas within the organization that are currently at higher risk of disunity. Once identified, strategies for engaging in productive conflict management and corporate visioning become means toward bridging diversity of thought and behavior.

Identify those areas of disharmony, disunity or heightened vulnerability within your organization:

_____

_____

- One means of bridging disunity and promoting the unity of the organization is to engage employees, board members and management-team members in the *exploration of the relevance of the corporation's mission* in light of the common good of society today. Conversations focused on the meaning and purpose of the corporate mission are best undertaken in small, heterogeneous groups comprising persons from all aspects of the organization. Care is taken that each member of the small group has the opportunity to share his or her perspective of the meaning and value of the corporate mission. The goal of such interaction is to serve as a reminder that there is value and dignity in the role each person exercises in the company. The *process* of engaging in conversations pertaining to the meaning of the mission is likely as important as any conclusions that are drawn from the interaction. Reflect on and talk about:

How is what we are doing as a corporation benefiting the society in which we live? What difference are we making, or do we want to make, in the world? How is my role abetting the accomplishment of this purpose?

- *Managing conflict* well is another means by which disunity is bridged within an organization. Effective conflict management is predicated upon certain assumptions, namely:

  - competent facilitation by a professional who is disinterested in the outcome;
  - rigorous, advanced preparation for the discussion;
  - a willingness to learn from others;
  - an atmosphere of mutual respect;
  - investment of all parties in achieving greater understanding and in arriving at a method for proceeding that will benefit the greatest good of the organization and the publics that it serves;
  - relinquishment, on the part of each person involved, of the need to have personal opinion prevail;
  - commitment to stay in the dialogue to its conclusion.

What are significant areas of difference of opinion within your organization that you believe must be addressed to link spirits on behalf of the common good of all?

How might *not* addressing these conflictual issues interfere with corporate effectiveness?

Are you aware of potentially destructive conflicts within your organization or between your organization and other groups or individuals? If so, what can you do to disarm the conflictual situation?

- *Moving visionary directions to action* is another means of promoting the unity of the corporation as it strives to make a difference in the world. Visionary directions take firmest root in response to critical needs. Awareness of compelling need taps into our altruism, into our desires to make some impact with our lives. Whether these needs are initially identified in relationship to the company itself or in the company's relationship to the larger external reality, the spiritlinking leader possesses the ability to call the group to reflect on a reality larger than what is immediately evident. Many organizations spend countless hours in "visioning sessions." A real challenge to the viable corporation is the development of strategies for implementing visionary directions. It is common for groups to articulate visions that flow from an understanding of the corporation's cherished values and mission, but it is also common for these same groups to fail in the process of trying to move wonderful ideas to tangible actions. The jump from the bright idea to its concretization frequently falls short. Consider some steps to arrive at actions based on the articulation of a visionary corporate direction:

- Articulate the vision:

  · Identify the area of *critical need.*
  · Specify what new project, consistent with your organization's purpose and expertise, is being proposed to address this critical need.
  · Determine the degree of excitement among those participating in the discussion. (If there is little enthusiasm, abandon the idea!)

- Design the implementation of the vision:

  · Discuss why you should do this.
  · Who is willing to take responsibility for seeing that it is accomplished?
  · What networks need to be established in order to strengthen the effort?
  · How will others be engaged?
  · *What needs to happen next?* (No visioning session should end without this question being asked.)

- Evaluate the vision:

  · How does this vision give expression to our corporate "best self"?
  · What promise does it hold for addressing critical need?
  · What promise does it hold for us?
  · How might this foster partnering, community formation, networking?
  · Who is missing?

- Formulate the action plan:

  · What concrete steps do we need to take to realize the vision?
  · *Who* will do *what?*
  · Develop a time line.
  · Determine lines of accountability.
  · Establish a method for continuing evaluation.

What bold action, if undertaken by your company, could make a significant difference in the life of the company and in the lives of those whom it serves? Ask "Why *not* try this?" rather than "Why do this?"

Chapter 2

WORKING THROUGH RESISTANCE

Imagine for a moment the novice paraglider going out on his first sail. He anxiously looks forward to the extraordinary experience of floating on the winds and anticipates the adventure of being carried down to some imprecise and yet unexplored landing place thousands of feet away. Prior to his jump he is asked to sign disclaimers that he knows this is a dangerous activity that could place his life at risk. He must evaluate whether the adventure is, indeed, worth the risk. Having made an initial decision to go through with it, he is then instructed to strap himself into the forward position of a two-person harness. A veteran paraglider is his partner and instructor, strapped in behind him. Now he is told by his instructor that they are to stand about a hundred meters from the edge of the cliff. From this point, the novice is told to set the pace, to run as fast as he can and, without breaking his gait, to leap off the edge of the mountain. His partner runs with him as together they must continue the running motion of their legs and feet as they are entering well into the open air.

If resistance grabs hold at some point in the process and is not immediately resolved, a number of consequences could present themselves: Fear could take over and the mission could be aborted before the harness is

ever secured; ambivalence could overtake the novice
partway through the dash, and he could turn around;
worse yet, panic could set in at the edge of the cliff, and
a dead stop could result in disaster as the veteran
pushes the novice headlong over the precipice without
the speed needed to catapult them away from the side of
the mountain. The most destructive thing a leader can
do is to ignore the power and the potential harm of
unaddressed resistance.

Resistance, in and of itself, is neither good nor bad. It is
an *unconscious* process of retarding or blocking the
process of transformation. No group or individual can
withstand unimpeded change. Resistance serves the purpose of allowing an organism to consolidate its gains as it
internalizes changes it has undergone. When resistance
remains routinely unacknowledged, however, it obviates
the revolutionary change organizations must face in a
rapidly reconfiguring global environment. Unaddressed,
resistance furiously tries to withhold and contain the emergence of the new and unknown. In any living organism
faced with the prospect of changing, resistance will surely
be present. What may not be readily apparent is that resistance intensifies as transformation becomes more
inevitable. The closer the organization comes to radical
revisioning in fidelity to its mission, the more rigorously it
resists it; that is to say that organizational change does not
occur simply because change seems like a subjectively
good idea. Transformative change becomes imperative
because the changing environment demands it. For example, a mission-driven corporation desires to provide better
service, address an unmet or critical societal or environmental need, or to extend care to a previously ignored sector of the population. Its leaders know that yesterday's
strategies are insufficient to meet the expectations of effec-

tive performance today. The organization is led into the daunting task of transformation precisely because it is alive to the needs of the environment in which it is situated.

Organizations that will continue to be successful are those that are hypervigilant to the signs of the times. As the needs of a rapidly changing global system escalate and reconfigure, these organizations place themselves at the intersection between structured order and random chaos. They maintain sufficient inner continuity and consistency to sustain the high degree of creative risk taking that issues the surprises of previously unimagined possibility. But regardless of the conscious imperative and desire for such radical change, this is extremely uncomfortable space for any organization as well as for all the human beings that comprise it. When something is uncomfortable or potentially threatens one's security, the self-protective mechanism of resistance is triggered. People and organizations always resist transformation, just as no one readily seeks out the pain of conversion. Although spiritlinking leaders seek to envision and implement reengineering and redesign as they promote their organizations' fidelity to service, it should come as no surprise that they are met with the incalcitrant face of resistance at every step along the way. In no way does this signal willful, hostile opposition; it is simply part of every organism's natural response when its safety is in jeopardy. As excellent leadership draws an organization closer to the achievement of a transformed vision and the realization of the organizational mission, members begin to intuit the risks entailed as the heart of the mission is approached and they defend against the need to take those risks. Taking risks threatens familiar stability because risk always entails relinquishing some, if not all, of those behaviors that have been responsible for the organization's social success and economic viability in

"People and organizations always resist transformation, just as no one readily seeks out the pain of conversion."

the past. The very predictability and familiarity of those business practices, along with their record of achievement, make them particularly difficult to abandon. Put another way, the organizational psyche begins to anticipate the grief and anxiety that permeate refounding change as it demands such pervasive letting go. The result is the intensification of resistance.

Any venture into the untried and the previously unknown is frightening because it threatens the comfort of having things under control. Equally disturbing, it places failure within the realm of possibility. Understandably, entering into any new space gives rise to resistance, despite all the best intentions of individuals and of groups to move forward. Simply put, resistance occurs when one becomes fearful of confronting imminent loss, fearful of facing an invitation to do things once thought impossible. Anxiety, frustration—even terror—can assault when one is confronted with that which is awesome, unknown and beyond clear control. Faced with the enormity of the turmoil and ambiguity that this era is generating, it is to be expected that organizations will engage in numerous resistant behaviors in their efforts to contain the anxiety inherent in facing the threat of the unknown. In some cases, engaging in behaviors that promote organizational transformation may seem as foolhardy as paragliding is to a settled midlifer. Consequently, the personal and corporate management of resistance is an essential skill for the spiritlinking leader so that potentially disastrous outcomes can be avoided. A successful outcome depends on people having a fair degree of trust in the leader's ability to maintain sufficient safety in the midst of a perilous situation.

Leaders must be able to recognize the presence of resistance, its purposes and its origins, as well as the consequences of its operation in the life of an organization. Those who understand this dynamic and the inten-

---

RESISTANCE:

An *Unconscious* Process Blocking Transformation

---

sity of the emotion that lies behind it have the potential to manage and work through resistance so that their organizations will move forward toward the profound transformative change that is a requisite for meaningful existence.

Static vs. Agitated Resistance

The lack of resistance does not portend a healthy organization. To the contrary, organizations that manifest little or no resistance in their corporate lives may be in extreme danger of calcification and ultimate demise. Apparently stable, low-conflict organizations that lack an agitated, high-energy interactional style are those in which leaders have left resistance unattended. The organization and its members have basically given in to complacent security and given up a will to be unsettled. Static resistance, where routine and the maintenance of current ways of doing business predominate, characterizes organizations in which security and past success have obviated the need for revolutionary change. The lack of networked communication, the preponderance of secrets and hidden agendas, the fear of retribution and punishment for deviating from the settled norm all suggest that static resistance has gained a strong foothold in an organization. Without realizing it, the process of organizational decay has begun. Curiously, often at highest risk are those groups that have enjoyed a markedly successful history. Cajoled by a sense of pride in a past well lived, these organizations live in the extreme of the prosaic adage, "If it ain't broke, don't fix it." The problem is that the "it" no longer holds relevancy. Agitated resistance, on the other hand, signals openness to the transformative process, even though that process is uncomfortable and disruptive.

A particularly dramatic example of these two types of resistance can be seen in the health care industry today. Consider a free-standing hospital that was founded decades ago in order to serve the needs of a particular community. Today it is faced with major strategic decisions about its survival. By design or by default, it has decided to continue to "go it alone," banking on past experience and the loyalty of the community it serves. Board members and management have participated in the enormous success of this institution and have shared in the pride of serving so well the health care needs of the community. While the financial picture has continued to be strong for the time being, tried-and-true constructs continue to be relied upon to seek increased financial productivity so that traditional ways of delivering service might continue. What this institution has been unable to do is to break out of an old way of thinking that proved extremely successful in the past. It may stave off the impact of the changing environment for a time, but resistance to revisioning, to breaking free from previously successful constructs, is ultimately going to take its deadening toll. Organizations like these are falling prey to a static resistance that is predicated on extraordinary past success. Unwittingly, leadership at the levels of the board and management has unconsciously colluded in institutional demise.

Many other hospitals today are exploding old constructs as they engage in turning inside out their understanding of their founding purpose and mission. Attention to illness is partnered with the promotion of wellness; healing is understood to encompass the body, the soul, the community and the environment, as well. Bricks and mortar are being replaced by information technology, which is rendering traditional forms of health care delivery obsolete. The primacy of the hospital is being replaced by the collaborative formation of comprehensive health care delivery networks designed as much to address the societal and environmental causes of illness as they are designed to promote healing. Openness to this massive shift in concept and operation gives rise to significant levels of anxiety at all levels of the organization. Agitated resistance is a well-known companion in these days of ground-shattering transformation. Management and boards that face nanosecond change and continuous agitated resistance and have developed a remarkable capacity to harness the energy generated by this chaotic state are leading these institutions. They have become expert at working through resistance. Although the health care industry is perhaps a clear example of how previous ways of doing business are no longer adequate to meet the needs of a global community in the midst of such a massive paradigmatic shift, all institutions are affected as the ground shifts beneath and the new paradigm attempts to emerge from the chaos. To deny this is to prepare for extinction.

Manifestations of Resistance

Organizations—and the people who work in them—attempt to bind the anxiety generated by unprecedented change by engaging in various unconscious maneuvers designed to protect them from the onslaught of change. Unconscious resistances serve as an apparent protection for any person or group faced with rule-fracturing change. It is crucial to keep in mind that resistance always occurs when organizations face a powerful invitation to transform themselves to respond with greater fidelity to their mission. Resistance can be identified through the deployment of defenses such as organizational isolation, projection, splitting, "doing" and "undoing", denial, rigidity and corporate depression. Anxiety typically serves as an overarching indication of resistance at work and, as such, is a helpful indicator to astute leaders that they should be on the alert for sources and symptoms of resistance. All resistances are directed toward making one feel safer and more protected. The more the emergence of the new and untried comes into organizational awareness and is experienced as a source of threat to its present ways of functioning, the more anxious the organization becomes and the more adamantly it will attempt to fortify itself against the perceived dangers arising from such a situation.

"All resistances are directed toward making one feel safer and more protected."

Fear causes groups to engage in behaviors that distance them from, protect them from and cause them to threaten other groups in much the same ways that fear causes nations to engage in war. What might be at the root of such fear? Feelings of anxiety often mask underlying, more basic emotions. One explanation for increased fearfulness is that it arises from significant feelings of group, or corporate, inadequacy. For certain, feelings of inadequacy have intensified in nearly every sector of personal and institutional life as external structures and defining characteristics of corporate identity have become less clear-cut today. With increased ambiguity, anxiety mounts. When a group experiences a loss of role clarity or is confused about its mission, it becomes more tempted to arm itself, perhaps quite covertly, against perceived impending crises of diminishment. It fights desperately to stave off the death of what once was. The more a group feels threatened, the more likely it is to become subtly armored against being intruded upon by another. Translating this dynamic, companies thus move away from collaboration, adopting instead isolationist, protectionist and highly individualistic strategies in the marketplace.

Reflecting on this as a metaphor that addresses the potential diminishment of global community, it is a particularly foreboding situation. It is within the realm of organizational power for corporations to engage in behaviors that will result in the fracturing of community and damage other dimensions of our global reality. Aspects of the potential for corporations to become a healing metaphor for our world will be explored further in Chapter 5.

Anxious times give predictable rise to various forms of defending against the onslaught of fear. Resistance serves such a protective purpose. While it is erroneous to interpret its presence as something necessarily "wrong" or "bad," it becomes noxious when it is not recognized. Resistance takes hold within any organization in the throes of overt or covert anger in the face of needing to let go of what has been familiar. When anger and anxiety remain unrecognized and resistance is, therefore, not managed, it will escalate, ultimately intensifying its presence until the organization is rendered paralyzed. To become more adept at recognizing the presence of unconscious resistance at work in an organization, it is helpful to consider some of its more common manifestations.

Isolation is a form of resistance that is called by many names. Its purpose is to interfere with the ability of an organization to engage collaboratively in alliances and networking, which will lead inevitably to innovation and

MANIFESTATIONS OF RESISTANCE

- Isolation

- Projection

- Splitting

- Doing and Undoing

- Denial

- Rigidity

- Depression

more effective response to the contemporary environment. Corporate self-sufficiency insulates the organization from having to reimagine itself in response to its purpose. Collaborative engagement, on the other hand, opens the door for the "risky-shift" to occur; that is, decisions undertaken in collaboration are likely to be more radical and more creative than decisions made by one entity acting alone. A risky-shift taken in direct counterstance to isolation occurred when two religiously sponsored health systems collaborated and merged to establish what has now evolved into one of the most creative and successful not-for-profit health care systems in the United States. Their initial risk—losing a sense of individual identity, letting go of old stories and taking on the task of writing a new one, relinquishing control and replacing it with the fiduciary role of influence—was undertaken only because of a common desire to care for the poor and most vulnerable. That sense of mission was strong enough to propel the two groups into an untried relationship that has continued to author new partnerships and forge new alliances with other health care providers, with housing initiatives and with environmental efforts. Key to this corporation's success and central to its capacity to work through resistance has been its fidelity to its fundamental mission question: How can we ensure the health of the most vulnerable in our society?

Alert organizations know that collaboration will indeed give expression to new vision in service of the mission. Yet to move beyond the seductive defense of isolation means the organization endorses risk taking and the grieving that necessarily accompanies it. Organizational cocooning serves as a defense against this, as it creates an apparent existence of self-sufficiency, self-focus and group comfort where the status quo remains safeguarded and the need to let go of past ways of going about business is postponed. In this way, the anxiety that the process of transformation generates remains bound for a time, and an illusion of security is maintained. At the same time, the moment for strategic action passes.

"...collaboration will indeed give expression to new vision in service of the mission."

Isolation serves as a manifestation of resistance in organizations as a whole, in divisions and departments within organizations, among individual employees at any or all levels of the corporate structure. Left unattended, it will intensify to a point where it ultimately will serve to abort every concerted effort toward timely revisioning. Isolation, by its very nature, moves an organization precariously down the slide toward decay proportionately as collaborative synergy has been denied.

Projection is the attribution of unwanted or dangerous desire, thought or feeling to another. It is often characterized by blaming and by other forms of externalizing responsibility for the situation at hand; that is, threatening material lodged in the core of the organizational self is ascribed to some outside source and experienced as issuing from that entity. For example, a mental health clinic is beginning to experience a downturn in viability. In its corporate "psyche" it is feeling increasingly ineffective. Employees exhibit low morale as salaries are frozen, but rather than engaging in the difficult process of radical redesign, management unconsciously postpones difficult action and blames the economy and the competition for the downturn. In turn, employees blame the clinic management. This behavior makes little cognitive sense as other clinics that share a similar mission are succeeding. Such blaming behavior is a clear signal that resistance is at work. When projection is operating in the life of an organization faced with transformation, leaders are frequently blamed for the disruption and the pain. Similarly, examples of projection are apparent in the manner in which the demands of the strategic plan are displaced onto an abstracted entity such as "corporate." In this way individuals purge themselves of the need to take responsibility for pain entailed in participating in the realization of transformative vision. Most successful businesses and institutions involve many people at various levels in the organizational structure in fashioning new visionary direction and strategic plans. Nevertheless, despite all best efforts to engage participation, it is not uncommon to hear telegraphed statements like, "Now what does 'corporate' want from us?" or "Whoever thought this up?" This frequently leaves leaders and board members bewildered as they recall the authors of the planning to be among those who are now most critical of it.

If projection is understood as a form of resistance arising from underlying fear of the consequences of participating in the realization of transformative vision, we can get a clearer sense of how to manage this apparent lack of ownership. What we are really hearing is something more akin to "I am irritated with myself for being so afraid to engage in this and for lacking the courage to try something very different." In an attempt to be rid of such uncomfortable feelings and thoughts, responsibility is projected onto another entity. Anger and blame effectively block the realization of the vision. Truly, one is unable to see well when blinded by rage.

Closely related to isolation and projection is the use of **splitting,** which unconsciously promotes the fragmentation of the organization through the establishment of factions of competing rather than collaborating divisions. The reason for the splitting resides in the attempt to deposit elsewhere, and thereby contain, the more threatening and demanding aspects of the transformative vision. For example, the central administrative team becomes the container for all that has engendered upset and discomfort in the company. The container for the threatening (i.e., visionary) elements becomes the locus for all that is "bad," thereby effectively splitting off from contact with the "good" (i.e., status quo). While some discomfort with authority is inevitable in human institutions of any sort at any time, splitting undermines relationships as it destroys well-intentioned efforts of colleagues. Obviously, such divisive behavior can have disastrous consequences for an organization. Splitting dynamics, left unchecked, can actually destroy institutional cohesion to such an extent that the organization is in danger of dissolution. The fallout for leaders can be profound as they experience themselves as the personification and container of the perceived threat. Unwritten histories of many organizations contain examples of executives and managers who have borne the personal pain of splitting dynamics. Splitting threatens the integrity of the organization. Stirring up opposing factions, engaging in gossip directed toward diminishing certain divisions or persons while aggrandizing others, and developing covert coalitions all signal the dangerous presence of splitting.

A faculty in a large university was confronted with the need to revise and reframe its core curriculum if it was to remain competitive and be successful in preparing its graduates to enter the marketplace. Necessarily, some courses were going to be dropped and faculty reassigned. Some faculty would be asked to assume new courses and would be expected to engage in new modes of instruction. One large department within the university began to call meetings of other faculty members during which the administration was severely criticized. Administration was seen as the reservoir of all that was malevolent. Plans were put in place to engage in organizing strategies directed toward sabotaging the changes. The faculty thereby was successfully divided as internal conflict consumed a large degree of the energy that would have otherwise been required to execute the innovation. It was not until an outside consultant was engaged that the resistant patterns were identified and explored and the process toward institutional self-harm averted.

Doing and undoing represents another common mode of blocking the process of transformation. Although aware that fresh vision must be realized, the organization becomes paralyzed and unable to move forward because it insidiously and cleverly "undoes" whatever actions it has undertaken to clear the way for revolutionary action. For example, a decision is made to partner with another organization because the overall good that is shared in common will be better served. But that decision is thwarted by circular discussions on process, methodology, the need for further study so that a mistake will not be made, debates about consultants and, ultimately, about the efficacy of the entire idea. In a common defensive maneuver, "process" is typically targeted as a manipulative and faulty attempt on the part of one subgroup to "control" the outcome. Banishing the facilitator becomes great sport in a group intent upon doing and undoing. Meanwhile, in the rest of the organizational arena, a business-as-usual approach to daily life is maintained, and the organization distracts itself from dealing with the future. Organizational anxiety has thus been sufficiently bound by this ritual of doing and undoing, and the organization continues to live with the illusion that everything is relatively under control. Sadly, the common good will not be well served, the mission will not be addressed in timely fashion and the transformative vision will have been compromised under a guise of furious and futile activity.

A sad example of doing and undoing took place in a large metropolitan area where two churches several blocks apart were faced with a challenge to expand their mission by opening their church halls to homeless people who were in danger of freezing in the cold northern winter. The parish councils met to make plans to initiate a comprehensive food-and-shelter program that would realize the best in ecumenical cooperation in the service of the poor. Contacts had been made for food contributions; lists of volunteers had been drawn up; the pastors of both congregations had preached to their people about the value of this concrete expression of charity. Seemingly, everything was in place and the program was set to begin until a member of one of the parish councils started to revisit the idea: "Shouldn't public agencies be doing this? If we do this, then we will offset the likelihood of the local government taking it on. Besides, we didn't have a thorough enough process for making this decision. It was too

controlled by the other church." With that, the undoing
process began. The winter became colder and the church
doors were never opened that year. The congregations
avoided engaging in action that could ultimately have
resulted in their communal conversion.

Denial represents the most primitive—and likely the
most dangerous—defense against transformation. Its result
is the irrelevancy of the organization in relation to its mission in the world. Denial assures the diminishment of the
quality of organizational life and the deprivation of its
future. It is a desperate attempt to protect the way things
are by negating the existence of any difficulties with the
present mode of functioning. Everything is just fine the
way it is. Denying any need to restructure or reenvision,
the organization engages in heroics as it attempts to shore
up its present modes of operation by pouring more
money into maintaining the present system of doing
things. As it bleeds from every orifice, it continues to ask
for transfusions. Emphasis is clearly on maintenance, not
on mission. Because of its commitment to maintain itself,
it deludes itself into thinking it is effective because it
appears very actively engaged.

Imagine hundreds of employees making certain that an
enormously complex machine is functioning well. Some
are cleaning and polishing its parts. Others are working
diligently to make sure its internal configurations are
accurate. Others are checking for defects. Still others are
ensuring that the workers are well cared for and that poli-
cies and procedures are updated. All are content in their
acknowledgment that everything is under control. The
only problem is that no one asks, "What is this thing and
what is it supposed to do?" Denial prohibits an organization from asking the question, "Who are we becoming
and what should we be doing in response to today's
needs?" In the failure to ask this, organizational death

comes rapidly. In a certain sense, denial represents a kind of terrarium mentality or an organizational reactionary fundamentalism by which smug self-satisfaction and self-righteousness negate the need for attention to the outside world. A terrarium with its lid on contains a lot of small plants in a self-sustaining environment. All the plants do well as long as the glass is kept on top of the container. The outside world is kept at bay and the inside world gets along fine. But plants in terraria never seed the outside world. Just don't take the lid off!

Rigidity represents a further attempt to resist the impact of transformation. Organizations that are comprised of bright, educated perfectionists who find it rattling to make mistakes and disconcerting to manage messes are at risk to be transfixed by this form of resistance. In an effort to contain the massive amounts of anxiety the advent of transformative change generates, the organization spends time designing tighter systems of control and accountability. Hours are devoted to examining how it might better proceed in the here-and-now. Operational procedures are reviewed and detailed extensively. Such extreme adherence to rules and procedures is indicative of the need to keep things under control. In this way, the imminent chaos and its messiness are avoided by fixing up and preserving tried means of addressing problems. Such rigidity bespeaks a futile attempt to control the radically shifting environment as outmoded internal structures are quietly crumbling. While seeking to protect the organization from profound redefinition, rigidity serves to snuff out its spirit. An organization's spirit exists primarily in the dynamism of the processes it undertakes as it struggles to mend the rift between the culture and the values and meaning it seeks to infuse into that culture. An organization's "soul" does not reside in forms created along the way.

"An organization's 'soul' does not reside in forms created along the way."

Rigidity speaks to a "circling the wagons" effort whereby a group attempts literally to brace itself for the onslaught of any eventuality. Little space can be left for creativity. Oftentimes in organizations struggling with this form of resistance, hiring decisions reflect its present dilemma: Cautious, predictable settlers are hired before innovative pioneers.

Resistance that is neither identified nor addressed gives rise to **depression.** While other segments of the global and economic environment continue to evolve, the organization stagnates. Therefore, corporate malaise manifested in complacency, low morale and loss of a sense of organizational meaning and purpose frequently blocks a group's energy to address the future. The phenomenon of the settled and satisfied reflects the weariness of the corporate spirit. It speaks to having lost heart and meaning. Such a loss of spirit results in the obviation of creativity and blocks the open spaces where imagination and vision are born. Critical to the identification of resistance in its varying forms is the ability to address it while it still bears its agitated quality.

Signs and Symptoms of Resistance at Work

On a concrete and practical level, leaders can recognize symptoms of resistance in day-to-day behaviors within the organization itself and in its responses and functioning in the marketplace. Symptoms of resistance may be indicative of either a static or an agitated inhibition of the process of organizational transformation. That distinction is made largely by determining the extent to which the organization is uncomfortable with what is occurring. An uncomfortable group, in other words, portends the imminence of transformative action. As the organization commits itself to moving forward toward the realization of its mission, it necessarily experiences intensified stress and heightened ambiguity in its decision making. Stress and ambiguity, in turn, give rise to resistant behaviors. As the group is able to assess—as objectively as possible—what is occurring in its organizational behavior, it frees itself to take action to work through the blocks to its continued trek toward transformative change.

Process of Working through Resistance

Given the pervasiveness of resistance in transformative times, the management of resistance is a required skill for any successful leader today. A major difficulty that has surfaced in many organizations is that although resistance is often recognized, leaders have not known how to work through it. Consequently, the process of transformative change has often been unnecessarily thwarted. Spiritlinking leadership entails attending to a deceptively simple fourfold dialogic process for managing resistance. It is, however, a process that cannot be short-circuited.

The first thing leaders must do is identify and articulate the manner in which the organization is evidencing resistant behavior. Naming the modes of resistant behavior provides an objective identification of organizational behavior that is observable and quantifiable. Interestingly, groups are seldom likely to name this for themselves. It thus becomes an obligation of good leadership to recognize and articulate for various entities within the organization the ways in which it is attempting to back away from the anxiety generated by the onslaught of change. Identification of the mode of resistance

	INTRAORGANIZATION BEHAVIOR	BEHAVIOR IN THE MARKETPLACE
ISOLATION	• Little departmental exchange • Cliques • Autonomous decision making • Little consultation	• Self-sufficiency • Disinterest in collaboration • Adamant "stand-alone" philosophy
PROJECTION	• Atmosphere of criticism • Blame other departments, managers, colleagues, authority	• Blame external factors for operational problems
SPLITTING	• Overaggrandizement or hostile devaluation of individuals or groups • Coalition building, covert strategizing prior to meetings	• Public devaluation of competitors
DOING/ UNDOING	• Obsessive concern about and fear of making a mistake • Inability to bring agenda items to closure • Criticism of processes used to arrive at decisions, consequent retraction of decisions	• Waffling on decisions relative to realignments, partnerships, mergers, etc.
DENIAL	• Pollyannish worldview • Oblivious to problems in the organization • Inability to manage discord	• Lack of attention to or awareness of market trends • Incognizant of emergent needs
RIGIDITY	• Preoccupation with policies and procedures • Resort to legalism • Self-righteousness • Dogmatism	• Heavy emphasis on tradition and history • Unwillingness to modify strategies, policies in order to collaborate with others
DEPRESSION	• Absenteeism • Attrition of key employees • Lethargy at meetings • Silence, lack of initiative and enthusiasm • Low energy level	• Public invisibility • Poor growth record

answers the simple question, "What's going on here?" It addresses that question without subjective interpretation and without judgment. For example, board members may note to management that the lack of timely decision making has resulted in missed opportunities that are jeopardizing the strategic positioning of the organization, or a manager may offer the observation to employees that participation in key meetings has recently been more subdued and there has been an increase in absenteeism. A CEO may point out to key staff that a certain issue has surfaced for discussion four times in the past week and that the issue is yet to be resolved. Pointing out the mode of resistance dispels the grip it stealthily holds on the organizational psyche. On the other hand, to make a subjective intervention such as "Some of you continue to hang on to this item and you are wasting precious work time. I wish you would stop it and let the rest of us make a decision!" heightens defensiveness and further entrenches resistant behavior in anger. The statement suggests that the participants are willfully interfering with the decision-making process.

The second task in the management of resistance entails encouraging persons to explore the underlying unconscious **motives** for the resistance. Leaders engage the group in examining responses to the question, "Why might this be happening *now?*" This is deliberately framed as a tentative query, posed to elicit possible underlying reasons for the resistant activity. Its tentativeness lowers defensiveness and allows greater risk taking in an articulation of hunches. For example, an exploration of responses might point to unconscious wishes such as wanting to avoid making a mistake or being reluctant to let go of comfort and predictability or needing to keep things under control. Employees may recognize the emergence of apprehension as they are faced with needing to realign departments or divisions, a situation that will cause changes in role descriptions, reporting procedures and accountability processes.

In the course of working through resistance to organizational transformation, it often befalls the leader to increase the pain. When organizational pain is sufficiently intense to the point of being intellectually and organically intolerable, transformative change becomes a real option. Pain is increased when the truth is told. To name avoidant organizational behavior and to begin a process for exploring its underlying motives increases distress. It would be quite wrong to suggest this is anything other than a very delicate process that demands a substantial degree of skill. In the best of all situations, leaders have sufficient adeptness to engage others in such an examination of the mode and the motive for blocking the process of transformation at this point in time. In the absence of a sufficient degree of personal comfort, however, good leaders may wish to engage the services of a consultant to assist in working through this part of the blockage. The essential skill is the ability to invite the investigation of the resistant behavior without laying blame.

Closely related to these two tasks and often concurrent is the corporate exploration of the **implications** of the resistant behavior for the future life of the organization; that is, what are some of the potential consequences for the organization if the resistant behavior continues to block the transformative process? For example, postponing decision making and failing to take timely action is likely to catapult the organization into a position of isolation. Nonparticipation at crucial meetings depletes creative imagination and may result in poor decisions being made based on the input of a few. Probing possible consequences for maintaining the resistant state of affairs is another way of increasing the pain. While not all the outcomes may actually come to be, colleagues have raised awareness of the dangers inherent in various "maintenance scenarios."

Fourth, given this examination of resistant behavior, leaders engage the members in exploring what they are willing to do together to move forward; that is, following the investigation of the resistant behavior, leaders ask the group to commit to **action.** No examination of resistance is complete without asking the question, "What are we willing to *do?*" A common error many leaders make as they attempt to manage resistance is to leap from the identification of the mode of the blocking behavior to the action needed to resolve the problem. This leap is always doomed to fail. It fails because the impetus for transformation arises from an organization's poignant awareness that it is no longer responding effectively to the needs it was once founded to address. To put it another way, the avoidance of the exploration of the motive and the meaning of the resistant behavior serves to insulate the organization from the acute pain needed to fire up the transformation process. When an approach of "Here's what we're doing to block change; let's stop it!" is undertaken, the behavior may actually cease momentarily. Predictably, however, it will reappear even more forcefully at the next turn in the bend.

"No examination of resistance is complete without asking the question, 'What are we willing to do?'"

Examination of the mode, the motive and the implications of resistant organizational behavior clears the way for action as it fosters community in the midst of turbulent moments. That which could never be surmounted individually becomes possible when persons feel connected to one another. Working through resistance becomes a means by which persons corporately begin to feel the excitement of approaching transformative vision and are willing to take the courageous steps to make it happen.

Spiritlinking leaders do not rid themselves or their organizations of resistance any more than they rid them of healthy conflict.

WORKING THROUGH RESISTANCE

The *Mode*:　　What is going on here?

The *Motive*:　　Why might this be happening now?

Implications:　　What are likely consequences if this behavior continues?

The *Action*:　　What are we willing to do?

Managing resistance, like managing conflict, does not obliterate it. Rather, a nonstagnating feisty resistance works through an organization like a three-dimensional spiral that continues its circling and intensifies its presence the more closely it approaches its conversion to the new and the untried. At each point, as the spiritlinking leader works to clear the way, the organization takes another step closer to realizing its mission in a new time. Agitated resistance is to be befriended as it signals an organization's commitment to keep faithful to its purpose in complex times.

Your Turn....

• Given your articulation of a visionary direction for your company and the beginnings of the formulation of strategic actions that can be taken to realize the vision, it is predictable that you and those who are faced with implementing these actions will fall prey to various resistant behaviors. Realizing that agitated resistance is always at work in any organization engaged in transformative change, it is important to take both a personal inventory of individual behaviors that may serve to block the realization of the vision as well as an inventory of corporate, management-team and employee behaviors that can impede the process of transformation.

Personal manifestations of resistance to change may include:

- procrastination, avoidance or postponement of action;
- diverting energy and attention away from the anxiety-inducing transformative task by focusing on more-routine and predictable agenda items;
- avoidance through illness or exhaustion;
- compulsive work or other compulsive activity not directed toward the transformative vision;
- obstructive behavior in group discussions, playing "devil's advocate."

Identify some specific resistant behaviors in yourself that surface when you are faced with engaging in risky, perhaps ambiguous, action directed toward personal and corporate transformation:

- Groups manifest resistance when they are confronted with the need to let go of past ways of conducting business and to move toward new ways that are focused on enhancing the organizational effectiveness.

Identify some practices or routines that your corporation needs to abandon in order to move more productively into the future:

A number of organizational resistances were identified earlier in this chapter. What behaviors do you note at work in your management team

as you attempt to abandon these practices? in your board of directors? among your employees as you attempt to relinquish some "old ways of doing business"?

Engage colleagues in conversation that explores possible reasons for these behaviors taking hold NOW. What purpose might these serve relative to the binding of anxiety in the face of transformative change?

- If these practices go unaddressed, a certain fact is that resistance will intensify until the organizational pain becomes so intense that one of two things must occur: Either the resistance will be worked through or it will result in the diminishment of the organization.

What actions could you and your colleagues undertake to move beyond the resistant behavior?

- Resistance can serve a beneficial purpose in protecting an organization from running headlong into impetuous changes. As a defense against making poor or impulsive decisions, resistance can slow the pace of change. There may be a temptation to generalize this insight in order to rationalize all forms of resistance to change; for example: "We can't take this on now because we have made too many changes already during this past year."

Can you identify a time when resistance to change served your organization well? How might you make distinctions between adaptive and destructive resistances in your work setting?

_____

_____

Chapter 3

SPIRITLINKING, TRUTH TELLING AND INCREASING THE PAIN

In a deep, underground cave in Slovenia, the Postojnska Jama, live strange albino amphibians that have never developed sight. Their skin is transparent and has a texture not unlike human skin. These so-called "human fish," or Proteus anguinus, *are living fossils. As the temperature of the cave and the water has remained constant over eons, these odd creatures have perfectly adapted to their stable surroundings, where there is no natural light. With no pigment in their skin and only vestigial eyes, they lack the ability to survive outside their environment—their skin has no tolerance for the light nor for any change in the temperature of the water they inhabit. The process of any adaptation to changing surroundings seems surrealistically paused as long geological periods have passed by their blinded eyes. To take these amphibians out of this predictable environment would be to cause them certain death. Even the artificial glow of the flashlights used to show them off to tourists has a deleterious effect on them. Consequently, the keepers of the cave must rotate the creatures to enable only the briefest moment in the purview of humans.*

Like these "human fish," there are corporations, institutions and organizations—even people—that have nestled into niches where they feel protected from any change in the environment, banking on the hope that no sunlight will intrude into their world, and, like these remnants of the fauna of the Tertiary Formation, they may serve no long-term purpose other than to be objects of anachronistic curiosity, souvenirs of a bygone day.

But the atmosphere is changing....

Truth telling invariably increases pain, as it is the first step in working through resistance. Truth telling is the basis for the identification of the *mode* of the resistant pattern. The psychological ramifications of the process of transformation demand serious consideration by those who lead. While every person has moments of longing for the security of the cave-dwelling preservationist, leaders who allow themselves to be deluded for a moment into believing that the pace of change will slow once redesign has been achieved, place their organizations in the same state of vulnerability as the *Proteus* who is placed in direct sunlight. Cave-keeper leaders take utmost care to insulate their organizations from the dangerous effects of light. Fearful of new vision they, too, have only vestigial eyes.

If attitudes toward personal conversion and the experience of organizational transformation and redesign are fraught with fear, anxiety and a sense of impending danger, organizations led by cave keepers begin to experience a loss of morale and flexibility. Such a depressive "tightening up" leads to a state in which the particular organization or institution ultimately becomes too rigid to adapt, lacking the passion to do more than maintain itself in the process of dying. This is the essential dynamic in any process of demise. Brittleness, whether it be emotional or systemic, leads to breakdown. Rather than relax their grip to allow for the refinement and development of expanded ways of thinking and responding, of questioning and evaluating, these leaders of institutions in the process of breaking down contract any remnant of visionary spirit as their organizations close in on themselves in a final desperate, protective act. Such organizations, along with their leaders, become fundamentally petrified, in both senses of the word: terrified, as well as rigid and lifeless.

Truth Telling and Disequilibrium

What they are unable to envision is the paradox of disequilibrium. In the very act of upset, of being thrown off balance, resides the potential for spirit to be transformed and creative innovation to take shape and find expression. Cognitive sets need to be disturbed in order for creative alternatives to be vigorously explored. New resolutions emerge as familiar processes and predictable environments become unsettled. What new creatures might have developed if gusts of fresh air unexpectedly whipped through that cave and shafts of light capriciously streamed into darkened recesses and warmed pools of water where the *Proteus* resided? Resilience just might have replaced organic vulnerability. Spiritlinking leaders encourage disequilibrium and overturn mind-sets by telling the truth about what is going on. It is this boldness that makes the difference between those organizations that will die and those that will find new energy, meaning and expression, for it is the act of faith through and in chaos, the belief in the energy of interconnection and fidelity to clear-eyed wonder, that organizational spirit is, indeed, set free to promote the good that the world holds in common.

Vulnerability, whether it be fiscal, personal or ecological, points to the need for transformation. It is well known

> *"Spiritlinking leaders encourage disequilibrium and overturn mind-sets by telling the truth about what is going on."*

that any major transformation in the history of civilization has been preceded by a variety of social indicators that highlight the extent of systemic vulnerability and throw the culture into disequilibrium. Painful expressions of unrest and social agitation signal the ineffectiveness of the present state. These include an intensification of feelings of alienation, an increase in mental illness, violent crime, transgressions of sexual taboos such as incest, rape and child abuse, social disruption, fundamentalist religious rigidity and the failure of long-trusted institutions. The prevalence of these indicators along with many others gives due warning to the vigilant leader that something needs to happen to reveal new visionary directions that hide just beyond sight. To believe that the unraveling can be halted or reversed is as delusional as thinking it can be ignored.

In What Ways Do You Experience Organizational Vulnerability Today?

Spiritlinking leaders are not afraid of the unpredictability of disequilibrium. Taking on the unpleasant but necessary task of increasing the organizational pain inherent in disrupting the status quo, these leaders realize they hold a key to determining the future of their organizations. What distinguishes them is their fearlessness in telling the truth. Truth telling and truth seeking obviously increase pain. They nudge organizations toward new light and a reclaimed and renewed spirit as their truthfulness throws their institutions into disequilibrium. Truth telling promotes disruption as it calls for heightened communication. The more communication, the greater the likelihood of divergent opinions. Truth telling and truth seeking inevitably create a condition of increased complexity. Truth pushes an organization beyond a state of equilibrium into a condition of overbalance, even unbalance, as old heresies of staid settledness give way to new paradigms founded on constant transformation. Even as truth telling increases pain, the spiritlinking leader knows there is no option. To promote the falsehood of stability will result in far greater pain as self-destruction takes hold.

Speaking the truth inevitably leads to challenge and confrontation. Leaders who risk this dangerous activity find their organizations increasingly questioning remnants of top-down modes of decision making and the exercise of authority at all levels within the organization. It is certainly no secret that autocratic, pyramidal systems are in decline and, daily, new systemic models are being developed that allow for efficiency, respect, ownership and mutuality.

Sometimes
The Leader's Most Important Task Is

to Increase the Pain

Leaders who tell the truth link spirits by promoting the shift away from an insular view of reality toward the interdependence that intensifies as decision making becomes more collaborative. Mechanized and often artificial divisions of labor promote closed relationships and heighten destructive conflict. Rigid, centralized structures crumble as persons recognize the disempowering and disenspiriting effect of systems that rely on control by a few. But movement toward responsible decentralization, in concert with flexible centralized processes, beckons toward profound relinquishing of possessiveness and ego. The challenge is how to maintain a strong organizational identity with increased team management in more decentralized organizational systems.

"Mechanized and often artificial divisions of labor promote closed relationships and heighten destructive conflict."

Cave Keeping

In the early 1970s, a small group of people embarked on the building of a not-for-profit organization with a mission of serving as a catalyst for positive changes in the lifestyles of North Americans of all ages. Their fledgling organization would provide education and experiences directed toward promoting balanced and healthful living. By the early 1980s, this organization (HPO) had employed a staff of eighteen people in its Pacific Northwest headquarters, gained exposure through a well-recognized sports celebrity serving as its chairperson of the board and spokesperson for the health promotion organization (HPO) and had an active advisory board comprised of highly dedicated and creative members from across the continent. In addition to publishing an impressive array of books and other materials on how to adopt a more healthful lifestyle, the organization published a bimonthly magazine and held annual conferences that addressed topics such as designing an exercise and fitness regime, reducing the risks of ingesting toxins, enhancing personal relationships, growing spiritually, coping with stress, making time for recreation and exploring holistic medical alternatives.

In response to member requests, a year-round healthful living workshop series was instituted to include yoga and meditation weekends, couples retreats and wilderness weeks for youth at risk, as well as classes on how and why to eat lower on the food chain, growing fruits and vegetables without pesticides, macrobiotic cooking and starting a community garden. Additionally, as a way of integrating the education and experiences into neighborhood communities, families and businesses, members formed affiliate organizations in twenty-six new locations, each of which was tailored to the perceived needs of that particular community and the specific interests and skills of the volunteers spearheading the local efforts. While an affiliate organization in the Midwest chose to focus on educating young people on alternative eating habits in direct contrast to the traditional food group pyramid, an affiliate in the East chose to direct its energies to a six-session workshop on stress reduction techniques.

Nationally, as well as in local communities, this mission-based, constituency-driven organization was flourishing. Its membership had been on a steady incline during each of its first ten years—its niche was readily identifiable and timely—its vibrancy was apparent.

But the atmosphere was changing....By the mid '80s most of the continent had become well aware of the benefits and attributes of healthful living. People had been bombarded with information, and options to support these enhanced lifestyle choices had become abundant. The uniqueness and value steadily diminished for this once progressive organization. HPO had become extremely vulnerable. Its CEO and central management team had become fearful of things getting out of hand. They feared loss of control. Consequently, without the conscious decision to sustain and promote disequilibrium and transform the organization to meet current and anticipated needs, this organization dedicated to healthful living began a decade of reactionary entrenchment without acknowledgment of its own deteriorating vital signs.

Programs were continued or eliminated based solely on their current financial sustainability, with no regard for their significance to the mission and without creative exploration of financial options. The community-based affiliate programs for volunteers remained, but rigid guidelines and prescribed projects replaced the flexible structures that allowed for customized programs in response to community needs. Publishing projects were reduced to the issuing of a quarterly newsletter for members. The only other program to be continued was the annual conference. By the early '90s, as organizational leadership maintained a facade of balance and stability, seventeen of the eighteen staff members were terminated the week following the annual conference, and the executive director was replaced with an acting managing director. Subsequent years brought financial woes evidenced in a glut of back taxes owed and a series of "loans" from the sports celebrity who had once represented the organization with passion and enthusiasm. Yet, leadership continued to assure everyone that "all is well" and that the organization was merely "consolidating its gains," a phase that, as the board and chairperson announced, was critical to the implementation of its blueprint for the future. Corporations, other not-for-profit organizations and numerous members surfaced with proposals to become part of the solution, but for the better part of the ensuing five years, their good intentions were met with a reaction from management that there was no problem and therefore there was no need for a solution. Despite the efforts to squelch these divergent discussions, members were energized by many of these ideas, alliances were built and several programs, projects and organizations took root outside the organization. Experiencing a loss of what had been, a frustration with what could be, and an escalation of negative emotions compounded by the knowledge that no one was focusing on what was going to be, by the mid '90s membership had declined to 10 percent of its healthier era.

What had been begun by a charismatic sports celebrity and a strong, centralized management group began to flourish even more extraordinarily as it moved toward more decentralized modes of realizing its overall mission. Membership was passionate, and enthusiasm and creativity were high, but fear of the loss of centralized control and an inability to maintain a clear, corporate identity and mission resulted in HPO's destruction. Had the management team been able to devise models for networking regional teams to each other and to the central management team, the future would likely have been much different. It is also important to note, however, that had HPO central management simply abdicated their leadership role in favor of unfocused decentralization, the organization would likely have disbanded at the same rate it did under unimaginative overcontrol.

The HPO case serves as a metaphor for numerous organizations that are finding themselves somewhere along the slippery precipice of diminishment, attrition and decline. Whereas growing movements, groups and individuals display an almost endless resiliency, versatility and enthusiasm, those in the process of disintegration exhibit uniformity, caution, lack of inventiveness and a corporate mourning over the loss of what once was. This is accompanied by a loss of internal harmony, depletion of morale and heightened internal discord. Truth telling stands in

"Truth telling stands in courageous opposition to the magnetic enticement of stability."

courageous opposition to the magnetic enticement of stability. It could have saved the mission of HPO and, in so doing, cleared the way for HPO to continue to make a creative and valued contribution to society. The very act of truth telling inoculates the leader against easily falling prey to promoting such deadly patterns that serve to promote artificial balance and stability. Denial, paralyzing anxiety, pathological grieving and rigidity are classic ways in which leaders avoid the truth and unwittingly promote institutional decay.

Attempting to Keep Balance

As it has been stated previously, denial is the antithesis to the transformational process. When organizational upset is not feared, the process of transformation can continue. However, the blatant denial of the changing environment, along with the skittish apprehension over the unavoidable disruption in the status quo at HPO resulted in the intensification of an isolated and insulated organizational style. HPO was simply "consolidating its gains" as it entrenched itself in the present and tried futilely to protect itself from the onslaught of change. As a dangerous, primitive defense, denial always results in the diminishment of life. It represents an unconscious attempt to escape from the pain and the vulnerability that comes from walking out into the bright light. Leaders engage in denial as they delude themselves into believing that their organizations will arrive at a stable, long-term resting place.

The illusion of stability was promoted by insulating the members of HPO from the dangerous effects of the light of new vision. If its leaders had been willing to promote cognitive upset and disequilibrium by engaging in a truthful dialogue about the situation, many financial options and opportunities for the organization to further its mission would likely have emerged.

Leaders who fall prey to paralytic anxiety as a defense against the disruption nested in transformative change are unable to engage in competent decision making. Moreover, they are unable to involve others in participative processes that move toward creative reimaging. Incapable of taking action to promote transformation, they are frozen into inactivity. Some regress to a passive-dependent state in which they rely on others to act on their behalf. Others are plagued by hidden desires to regain control. Paralyzed by fear, they are unable to open themselves to conversion, unprepared to clear the way for organizational redesign. Paralysis takes hold when power struggles emerge and are left unaddressed.

In HPO the sports celebrity and the board became transfixed by their inability to commit to a unified direction. The celebrity was intent upon maintaining a high profile in HPO in order to bolster his fading notoriety. The board felt compelled to revamp governance to accommodate a more decentralized organization but was unable to prevail. In a particularly telling and sad depiction of organizational pathology, it was rumored that the celebrity had "bugged" the boardroom as board members went into executive session to discuss the future role of that celebrity in the organization. Anxiety and fear had blossomed into full-blown paranoia. Paranoia and ambivalence resulted in time lost. As if this were not enough, HPO was further triangulated as organization members as well as corporate and nonprofit sponsors were greeted with skepticism and perceived by the board and the celebrity as unwelcome intruders injecting new ideas and plans for renewal and transformation. When paranoid behaviors—such as inveigling colleagues covertly to monitor and report on one another, or asking them to judge another colleague's fidelity to the organizational mission—become operant in the organization, it has entered into a critical stage of demise. Paranoid behaviors incorporate enormous amounts of pent-up rage and vengefulness.

Another effort to maintain equilibrium, skew the truth and stop the process of organizational transformation is pathological grieving. Leaders caught in this defensive posture portray a sense of futility, despondency and loss of faith in the group they represent. They are consumed by the prospect of failure and the lack the energy to become involved in the creation of the new. This response is most clearly identifiable in a loss of hope and a lack of belief that in the chaos of disequilibrium creative options will, indeed, burst open.

Unresolved grieving of leaders and members led HPO further down the path to ruin as the organization became increasingly depressed. Grieving over the loss of stature as a frontline herald of healthy living strategies, HPO first attempted to recapture its position by aggressive marketing strategies. But the field was now glutted, as the need was being addressed with apparent adequacy, and HPO's membership continued its decline. The celebrity chair's loss of prominence in the sports world added to the quiet depression that insidiously held the organization in a state of malaise. Attrition of membership continued at record speed. Few seek to join a depressed group or remain with one. Unwillingness to accelerate the letting go of what was no longer addressing its mission and failure to contend with the healthy grieving that necessarily accompanied the loss of what had become irrelevant led HPO toward stagnation. Long months of inactivity passed by eyes that had only limited sight and no vision.

Corporate rigidity is another means by which organizations and their leaders attempt to contain the massive amounts of anxiety that the potentially transformative situation generates. They form tight systems of external controls and often react with increased legalism. The slightest deviation from routine is interpreted as disruptive and judged intolerable. The underlying delusion is that by keeping the environment under control, the breaking down of outmoded internal definitions and ways of engaging in a transformed institutional mission can also be contained.

A bold component of the founding vision of HPO in the '70s was its parenting numerous community-based affiliate groups. Each group was managed locally by volunteers who designed, instituted and managed their own community-based programs. Fearful that diversity and decentralization would result in the loss of control, the board and the celebrity chair instituted rigid controls on affiliate programming. Projects were dictated by the central organization board instead of continuing to be born of member passion and community need. The healthy tension between flexible, centralized systems and creative, decentralized expressions of a corporate mission and vision had snapped. Apathy grew along with the membership's confusion, finally culminating in an escalation of anger. As a result, community-based initiatives ceased in more than half of the initial affiliate endeavors over the course of four years.

Exploring a Spiritlinking Alternative

Transformative change continues as long as spiritlinking leaders promote truthful responsivity to the mission. Telling the truth about what is going on is the first requisite for working through the predictable organizational resistance to change. The honest responsivity of truth telling continues to generate a momentum that carries the institution beyond a state of equilibrium and prevents sad outcomes like that of HPO. Had anyone in a leadership role at HPO had the courage to identify the problem and enlist the assistance of a consultant to work with the organization through its denial and disillusionment, the resistant posture would not have become so deadly.

During any time of disintegration, those who point to emerging constructs are often treated like alewives—met with disdain, perhaps with mockery and attempted suppression or annihilation, angrily attacked for their seemingly heretical proclamation that tradition must be redefined, if not wholly abandoned. For HPO to have continued its important mission of health promotion into the '90s and beyond, its leadership needed to engage in the uncomfortable and disquieting act of truth telling: that the mission is being adequately addressed by other groups; that HPO is no longer on the frontier of health promotion; that the organization is losing money; that all is not well. But signs of hope must accompany difficult news. Effectively addressing the resistance to transformation, the spiritlinking leader captures hope and rekindles passion by engaging others in processes of creative exploration of new ways of implementing an important mission.

As a service organization, HPO's fundamental mission was to better the quality of life. Passion is kindled when groups begin to explore questions such as: What are the unmet critical needs that cry out for attention so that a healthful future may be realized for future generations? What one need captures HPO members' energy? What action needs to be taken in order for this critical need to be addressed? Such questions cannot be explored well without the participation of a representative group of some of the most diverse and creative thinkers in the organization. The greater the diversity of such a think tank, the more probable a passionate redefinition will emerge.

In HPO, leadership had been in place too long. The founding time had passed when a charismatic celebrity could hold the organization together. The board had become too predictable and unimaginative. A broadened base of organization ownership had to replace one individual's founding vision. Others had to be empowered to carry the mission forward in new ways as more decentralized and participative forms of decision making and the exercise of authority replaced the wonderful talent and good will of the founders. There comes a moment in every group when it is time for the leader to step aside and let the new be born. The spiritlinking leader—in management as well as in governance—monitors ego and remains acutely attuned to subtle indicators that it is a new moment, a time to move on.

HPO needed to acknowledge and celebrate the marked contribution it had made in awakening North Americans to the option of a more healthful lifestyle, just as much as it needed to be emancipated from its successful past. Its leaders needed to help HPO members grieve the loss of something wonderful. Healthy grieving recognizes the wonder of the past and is a continual reminder of the certainty of ongoing conversion and transformation. In the upset of healthy grieving, the organization's heart is disencumbered and its passion is freed, once again, to find new expression.

Wonder in the Midst of the Mess

Common wisdom purports that the new paradigm will arise from the escalating foment that pervades today's reality. Chaos theorists assure that as disequilibrium is promoted and as perceived chaos increases, a self-organizing principle—call it spirit—takes over, and the new unexpectedly unfolds itself. *Chaos* is not synonymous with *disorder* or *randomness;* rather, it is a word used to describe a whole "science of process rather than state, of becoming rather than being."[3] The difference between disorder and chaos is that hidden in the midst of chaos is an extremely complex order that is often elusive until its patterns are ready to be manifested before human eyes and minds. The insights from mathematicians, physicists and biologists are extraordinarily profound and supportive of a faltering faith in the midst of the various apparent dilemmas in which one finds oneself these days. Acknowledging the import of chaos and promoting disequilibrium can be hard to comprehend or may perhaps be perceived as naive. It is likely, however, that many individuals have experienced an analogous phenomenon without knowing how to name it. Most of us can relate to being involved in a conflictual or baffling situation, perhaps a time when hours were spent poring over a problem and engaging in conversations and meetings that seemed endless. In the midst of fidelity to the mess, a surprising insight suddenly developed that markedly highlighted the direction to proceed.

> "Chaos *is not synonymous with* disorder *or* randomness...."

Things needed to get messier before they became clear. Sometimes the most important act is to be faithful to the chaos, with deep belief that an exquisite new order will soon become apparent. In the midst of chaos, upset and disequilibrium, leaders and their organizations may feel much like the *Proteus,* possessing only vestigial eyes. In the communion of others, vestigial eyes find sight, and fresh air gives expression to new creation.

Your Turn....

* Truth telling encompasses both good news and difficult insights. Leaders err when they fail to acknowledge directly individual and corporate successes and focus primarily on problems. All groups need to celebrate achievements. As futurist Joel Barker has said upon many occasions, however, those organizations that have enjoyed a markedly successful history often have a far more difficult time changing. Truth telling can assist in unlocking the grip of a successful past. By bringing to consciousness the historical good news, by acclaiming achievements and by reflecting on how those achievements addressed an important need at the time, leaders loosen the hold these successes have on present practices. Excellent communication and its contribution toward the establishment of an atmosphere of mutual trust is far better grounded in affirmation than it is in negative criticism. This is equally true for individual relationships and corporate relationships. Given this, consider:

What has been the "success story" of your organization?

_____

_____

As you look toward the future, what external events might already be jeopardizing your company's continued success in the areas you have noted above?

_____

_____

What are some hard truths your coworkers may need to become more aware of to explore new ways of entering the marketplace?

_____

_____

Chapter 4

LEADING FOR THE COMMON GOOD

On one extraordinary day in July 1997 a microwave-oven-size machine landed on Mars—right where it was supposed to land. It operated just like it had been programmed to act; basically, it performed flawlessly. On Earth, a team of scientists literally jumped with joy in the Jet Propulsion Laboratory as they realized that their vision had given expression to a mission that was accomplished. What happened was beyond their dreams. This team of individual experts was jubilant as together they realized that their hard work and their collaboration offered us earthlings a chance to see another world. They were passionate. They did something fantastic and offered it freely to the world as millions of us plugged into the Internet and participated in the unfolding events. The rock scientist was a master in his work; the computer technologists, physicists, troubleshooters, mathematicians and astronomers, each superb. During televised press conferences, each routinely deferred to the team member best qualified to respond to the reporters' questions. In simple humility, they knew clearly that, regardless of their skill, not one of them could have gotten to Mars without the collaboration of the rest of the team. They were able to accomplish their mission because their individual expertise was placed in concert with the rest of

*the team, and they achieved something far greater than
any of them had fathomed.*

Spiritlinking leaders want to see their endeavors make a
difference. They want to see something wonderful come
from all of the hard work of the women and men who
make up the company. They, too, long for the unimaginable excitement and passion that come with the knowledge that something important has been achieved as a
result of dreams and visions, commitment and hard work.

Any person who is called to be a spiritlinking leader
today is also called to the heroic act of unifying a group of
dedicated individuals in the midst of a world increasingly
fragmented and torn apart by individualism, nationalism
and regionalized separatism, in the midst of a corporate
world founded on competition and governed by principles
of globalization in which the weaker are frequently forgotten. At the same time, these leaders are cognizant of the
mounting connection of all dwellers on this planet. Insights
from world religions, the new sciences and feminist consciousness are continually shaping the actions of responsive and responsible organizations and businesses to the
suffering oppressed. They are also aware that a persistent
resistance to networking for the greater good represents an
intransigent block to entering into a viable future.

In the midst of a continuing escalation of complexity in
all institutions, companies and systems within which we
work, there is a concurrent, increasing diversification of
services within many organizations. In and of itself, this is
neither good nor bad. At issue is the ability of leaders to
maintain clarity about the mission and purpose of the corporation as it seeks to serve the global common good.
While there is an expanding impact of first-world globalization on developing countries' economies, there is also
indication of an increasing corporate awareness and

desire to withdraw from participation in those structures and systems that are oppressive and demeaning to those who are less fortunate. Similarly, there is some movement on the part of large corporations, as well as in the not-for-profit sector, toward collaborating with systems that address the needs of the poor, the oppressed and the abandoned across the globe. Leaders and employees alike are increasingly questioning the meaning and the consequences of what their organizations are engaged in and how this ultimately will affect the planet.

While levels of employee competence increase daily, leaders struggle with how this relates to developing a sense of collaboration, pride and communitarian accountability. A sad scene unfolds when management teams—perhaps in misdirected efforts to be liked by their employees—fail to critique emergent societal and cultural movements as these impact on the common good of their organizations or companies and fail to critique the impact of their corporate mission and organizational behavior on the common good of society. Ultimately, this leads to the common good being held hostage by malaise and a depletion of corporate passion. The common good is additionally in danger of becoming compromised when leaders have become overly confident in their organizations' current modes of functioning and have become lulled into a cognitive set that lacks sufficient imagination to develop new ways of doing things. Because the past has yielded enormous success, leaders experience less pressure to change and, consequently, divert their energy and attention from the compelling and potentially transformative task. Recall what occurred in the '70s in the U.S. automotive industry as efforts and finances were continually intensified in building more comfortable and larger cars. Meanwhile, in Japan, resources were directed toward the research and design of smaller cars with low energy consumption and low maintenance. Practices from a successful past were no longer adequate to meet the needs of the day, and the United States faced a serious challenge to its leadership in the global automotive industry. In an entirely different arena, the Catholic Church is facing a similar threat to its historical foothold in Latin America because fundamentalist sects are making far greater inroads in evangelization. In both instances, a certain confidence in past performance and relevance limited creative response to the present-day situation.

The common good may unsuspectingly and unwittingly be co-opted when leaders become frightened and paralyzed in the face of trying to maintain a competitive edge in the marketplace. They have become deaf to innovative voices because of their past successes and have thus enmeshed themselves and their organizations in resistance.

Spiritlinking leaders intensify their conviction that pluralism and diversity must be held in tandem with a binding sense of corporate identity and relationality solidified by strong, systemic core values and concerted goals. They know that interdependence is imperative for our survival as a planet, as nations and as relevant companies and organizations, and they are clear about the given that all living systems are characterized by networks of relationships. They are aware, more than ever, that everything we do and everything we produce is somehow connected and has an impact, for good or bad, on everything else. Consequently, they have learned that connections to and within the larger global community are necessary for responsible stewardship.

These excellent leaders know that neither hierarchic leadership models nor totally consensual models are effective in this time of rampant change, heightened complexity and anxiety-provoking ambiguity. Neither the subordination of individuals to the needs of the corporation nor the subordination of the common good to the needs of individual employees will make for a viable future. New expressions of stronger community in the workplace are being called for, whereby persons exercise true interdependence, participation and responsibility about matters pertaining to the well-being of all those systems of which they are a part.

Consider two midsize community mental health agencies, each founded about twenty-five years ago, each with a mission to provide quality mental health care to persons within their specific catchment areas. BetaCare grew as a traditional, top-down enterprise. By its twenty-fifth anniversary, it maintained a staff of eighty full-time employees. It was managed by a chief executive officer (CEO), an executive vice-president (EVP), a chief operating officer (COO), a chief finance officer (CFO), a vice-president of marketing, a vice-president of medical services, a vice-president of clinical services, a vice-president of community outreach, a director of intake services, a director of research, a director of communications, a director of support services, a director of housekeeping and a director of maintenance. Each director reported to a vice-president; each vice-president reported to either the EVP, COO or CFO; each of the latter reported to the CEO. Other than those who reported directly to her, the staff rarely set foot in the CEO's office. Generally, all strategic decisions were made by the CEO, EVP, COO and CFO, using conventional consensus techniques, which were undeniably reflective of the expressed or unexpressed preferences of the CEO. The senior management group prided itself on its lack of disagreement. Individual employees worked hard at their jobs as they tried to meet the demands of increasing needs and decreasing funding. In light of the sustained environmental pressures however, one by one, senior level clinicians began to resign from BetaCare in order to enter into private practice or small independent group practices with other former BetaCare employees. They believed they could earn the same or better salaries and exercise greater creativity in their work. Because they had little connection with the CEO and senior management members, there was no compelling affective pull to keep them connected with the organization. Furthermore, there was little innovative corporate action on the horizon. Very simply, work had become too routinized, with little passion and even less creativity.

Several hundred miles away, the CEO of the PsiNet community mental health agency had abolished the traditional organizational chart, along with most of the positions that went with it. Vertical reporting was replaced by an intricate system of networked teams with overlapping membership constellations. Each team selected a team leader to convene the work of the group and to hold the team accountable for carrying through what it had determined to do. The CEO periodically joined various teams to assist in the work at hand. Interdisciplinary treatment teams met for peer consultation; professionals in specific mental health disciplines met within their teams for ongoing in-service education; the research team explored critical questions that could shed light on procedures with the potential to enhance emotional well-being in the catchment area. The administrative team took care of daily operating concerns, finances and marketing. All eighty-three full-time employees, regardless of their organizational function, were on a first-name basis with each other. As critical issues arose, all teams with any insights on a particular situation were gathered to brainstorm possible strategies for addressing the crisis. In the absence of clarity concerning the resolution of a particular problem or crisis, a modified consensual model was used; that is, after considerable brainstorming and discussion of various possibilities, employees entrusted the refinements of the decision making to the CEO and appropriate team leaders. Work demands were high, with the same budgetary and census obligations as were evident with BetaCare, but loyalty, trust, morale and corporate pride were equally high. Renowned senior practitioners from across the region were eager to associate with PsiNet. Staff attrition remained low.

Perspectives on the Common Good

There are two mainline perspectives about how the good for society should be achieved. The first and more prevalent perspective is that this common good is achieved by each individual pursuing his or her own self-interest, the aggregate of which will then constitute the most good for the greatest number. Each employee does her or his job well and receives a salary increase, and the company expects to make a profit. This individualistic and utilitarian approach, spearheaded by John Locke, Adam Smith and John Stuart Mill, emphasizes the common good as a composite of individual goods. Clearly, North American organizations have historically reflected this more libertarian notion of the common good. BetaCare is an example of this model of commitment, whereby each person in the organization had, as his or her core desire, the pursuit of various personal interests, and each operated within the framework of a particular job description. It was sincerely believed that the sum total of these individual initiatives would bring about the best results for the company and, secondarily, for the public which it served. Good work, but no one gets to Mars.

The second perspective, coming out of the Thomistic tradition, emphasizes the common good as a social good in which all must participate if the good of the whole is to be achieved. Jacques Maritain further elucidated this when he spoke of a "personalistic communitarianism" in which persons are enabled more fully and readily to achieve their own goodness when they are in relationship with others toward the enhancement of the common good. In this paradigm, employees are so committed to the mission of the organization that they are willing to subordinate competition to collaboration in the interests of achieving an even more effective outcome. Fundamentally, this is what happened at PsiNet. Similarly, at the Jet Propulsion Laboratory, each scientist simply deferred to the team member who possessed the greatest knowledge in the particular area that the journalists were probing at the time. Ego was subordinated to the common good.

Against the backdrop of these differing interpretations of what constitutes the common good, two extreme ways of leading must be avoided: namely, a laissez-faire individualistic philosophy that heralds each person as completely autonomous and independent; the other, a socialistic collectivism in which the individual sacrifices everything for the organization, even to the loss of self-actualization. Neither BetaCare nor PsiNet reflected either extreme. Within these polarities, however, there exists a tension for leaders: to want each individual employee to find meaning in work and to be productive, and, at the same time, to want their institutions, organizations and businesses to unleash their communal potential in the service of society. If no individual NASA scientist had been recognized for the contribution that was made to the success of the entire mission, the individual would have been diminished in the sight of the communal effort. Similarly, if the accomplishment of the

NASA organization had not been recognized, the agency itself would have lost a sense of its identity as a mission-driven entity. At BetaCare, individuals did good work but had little tangible sense of the overall good that the agency was contributing to society. Corporate identity and pride were weak.

Spiritlinking leaders exhibit the competency needed to promote the societal good that is held in common and, at the same time, are able to safeguard the acknowledgment and affirmation of individuals. In other words, they know how to engender the same corporate passion and spirit in earthly endeavors like PsiNet as was engendered in the Martian mission.

Three areas of competency are necessary in order to achieve this: *conflict management, guarding against "groupthink" and promoting communal efficacious action.* These competencies call for particular attention today because a leadership team's proficiency in understanding the fundamental principles behind each of these competencies will help the organization to move forward while holding open the possibility of the emergence of true synergy. Synergy happens when a group is stunned by a previously unimagined resolution to a complex dilemma that arises from information-overload and from the incredible energy that inhabits chaos. Synergistic surprises emerge as the chaos reveals an inherent and exquisite order that was not previously discernible.

SYNERGY:

The Energy-Laden, Unexpected Accord

—or Communion—

That Emerges in a Group So That Momentum Can Be
Channeled toward the Good That Is Held in
Common

Becoming Comfortable with and Adept at Handling Conflict

Perhaps more than any competency needed by excellent leaders today is the ability to manage conflict well. In a real way, this ability short-circuits the likelihood of "groupthink" setting in and supports the promotion of communal efficacious action. Spiritlinking leaders know that conflict is a normal part of any human relationship and an important part of the interaction in any vital group. They also know that effective conflict management frequently feels counterintuitive. It flies in the face of our upbringing and our instinctive responses to confrontation, that is, *fight* or *flee.* We tend either to shy away from conflict altogether, take no action or procrastinate in the hope that the problem will go away; or we may engage in quid-pro-quo interchange; that is, we become defensive, fight back or engage in win-lose debate strategies. Inevitably, this leads to frustration, disillusionment and personal diminishment on both sides. With the flight strategy, we quickly learn that the denial of the possibility of conflict leads quickly to very destructive passive-aggressive behavior that eats away at the organizational gut. With the fight strategy, we find ourselves caught in dualistic thinking that categorizes others as either with us or against us, thus underscoring the proverbial line-in-the-sand with rather self-righteous, pretentious winners and demoralized losers.

PsiNet's CEO operated out of an alternative strategy. Continually, he modeled deliberately moving toward that which was difficult, disruptive or problematic in efforts to establish *human connection.* Members of networked teams disagreed with one another but were able to remain focused on the greater good for the agency and the people that it served. They seldom entered into personalized conflict. Team members met conflict proactively and anticipated confrontation as an opportunity to uncover the best possible solution to a critical situation. In so doing, the CEO and the PsiNet employees engaged in a solid process of ecological relationship building; that is, they were able to work through erroneous false assumptions and impetuous temptations to take superficial action and were thus able to foster healthy, life-engendering and respectful solutions for the community they served.

"Silence is a dangerously toxic way to break the spirit of an organization."

The excellent leader bears a serious challenge to take the fear out of conflict and, in so doing, to break open blocked lines of communication. Silence is a dangerously toxic way to break the spirit of an organization. It places the mission of the group in serious jeopardy. The spiritlinking leader knows that no topic can be off-limits for creative exploration.

Consider the paradox of prohibition. We say to a small child, "You may not, under any circumstances, open that closet door," or to a teenager, "You are absolutely forbidden to talk about that again!" Prohibition is always enticing and fosters defiance and sneakiness. The manager who says something to the effect of "I don't ever want to hear this topic argued about again" is assuming a parental role that will result in employees responding in anger, passive-aggressive behaviors and quiet rebellion. Difficult discussions engender uncomfortable, demanding and messy conflicts. But spiritlinking happens in the midst of the mess when persons interact as peers and commit themselves to stay in creative tension directed to the good that is held in common.

Spiritlinking leaders in this era of connection live in the midst of ongoing and predictable diversity and differences. Accordingly, they also live in the midst of the conflicts that arise from this plurality of insight and thought. Any successful engagement in conflict must be founded on certain assumptions: that there is a commitment on the part of all involved to learn from one another and to engage together in the search for truth; that there is an agreement to carry the conversation to its conclusion; that mutual respect among peers is a prevailing value; and that no party will resort to oppressive or vindictive strategies during or after the conversation. Those leaders who will succeed possess an internal disposition of flexibility, empathy, courage and creativity, as well as considerable mental inquisitiveness about the atypical and unusual. It is important to note, however, that even these qualities are insufficient if leaders themselves are frightened, unclear or noncommittal with regard to the fundamental mission and identity of the organization that they have been called to serve. In other words, if PsiNet's CEO was distracted from the overall purpose of the agency to provide quality mental health care for the people within the catchment area and, instead, began to promote the diversification of the agency into political action advocating for the rights of animals, the mission would have been compromised and the constituency harmed. The common good would have been transgressed.

CONFLICT MANAGEMENT

ASSUMPTIONS:

• Maturity and Psychological Health
• Dialogue among Peers
• Rigorous Study, Reflection
• Respect
• Commitment to Listen
• Relinquishment of Need to Convince, Win
• Agreement to Part as Friends

Similarly, spiritlinking leaders take clear and directed action to protect the solidarity of the organization and its commitment to unity in the face of challenges to its founding purpose, identity and mission. They do so by daring to gather the brightest, healthiest, most creative and strong-minded thinkers—with diverse backgrounds and perspectives—and set them to work on some of the most perplexing problems facing the organization. Toward the end of his struggle with cancer, Cardinal Joseph Bernardin, plagued by the prevalence of destructive factionalism in the Catholic Church in the United States, launched the Catholic Common Ground Initiative.[4] Designed as an effort to engage dedicated thinkers from all ideological positions in respectful dialogue on some of the more vexing questions dividing the Catholic community, the Common Ground Initiative is a striking example of a courageous, albeit spiritlinking, effort to stem the tide toward factionalism and separatism. Rather than fearing that they are setting the stage for perennial deadlock, spiritlinking leaders trust that the energy generated will result in far-more-exquisite solutions than those arrived at in the calm discussions of like-minded persons. Through competent conflict management, these leaders enlarge the circle of friends by engendering understanding through disequilibrium. They are not afraid of the confusion that ensues when massive amounts of apparently disparate information emerge. To the contrary, they welcome the wisdom and spirit of each participant and trust in the collective wonder of the group. Thus, truth is approached, and new energy pulsates in service of the common good.

Throughout processes of conflictual discussions, these leaders continually call the group to reflection about its mission, respectful engagement in dialogue and continued exploration of that mission in light of the needs of these times. They, with the members of their organizations, businesses or institutions, walk toward what is new and claim their truth in commitment to the greater good. In so doing, they free their companies and organizations from any grip of static resistance and challenge the visioning and realization of the yet-to-be.

Guarding against Groupthink

The greater the extent of ambiguity in a particular situation, the more likely it is for leadership teams to fall into what some group analysts refer to as "groupthink." This is a dangerous dynamic that arises when, in the face of adversity or perceived danger, a cohesive "in-group" (for purposes of this discussion, a management team) insulates itself from conflict with the "out-group," that is, the employees. It does this by concurrence seeking and unquestioning agreeableness among the in-group members. Groupthink resulted in BetaCare becoming a boring, unimaginative organization with very little creativity endorsement evidenced in any aspect of its functioning. Fundamentally, groupthink interferes with leadership's ability to act on behalf of the common good because it has closed off alternative courses of action. It falls into a tight-knit, closed system in which management team members avoid deviating from consensus. The in-group thus shares an illusion of unanimity concerning most of its judgments and positions. In the worst scenario, certain members of the in-group (leadership team) unwittingly assume the role of "mindguards" who protect the CEO and other in-group members from adverse information that might break their sense of well-being about the perceived success of their past decisions.

"...groupthink interferes with leadership's ability to act on behalf of the common good because it has closed off alternative courses of action."

Groupthink results, therefore, from largely unconscious efforts on the part of a management team to fortify
itself in ambiguous, conflictual times, against perceived
threats from the out-group. It is characterized by the in-
group feeling a certain invulnerability and overoptimism
about the future. This happens because negative feedback has been dismissed as a result of rationalizing and
stereotyping the behavior of the disagreeing others as
being invalid, irrelevant, erroneous, disloyal or unin-
formed. Leadership teams forfeit possibilities for excellent decision making in favor of group allegiance and
cohesion; that is, members of a management team caught
in groupthink unconsciously place a higher value on
being part of their own in-group than on arriving at the
best decision that will favorably affect the out-group and
the corporate mission. Concurrence, solidarity and
mutual liking outweigh rational decision making as information is processed in a dangerously biased manner. This
is a recipe for organizational and leadership mediocrity.
Research has shown that a factor differentiating excellent
leaders from average leaders is the capacity to subordinate
the need to be liked to the need to accomplish the organizational mission.[5] Paradoxically, when in-group unity and
unanimity are too strong, leaders run the risk of sacrific-
ing their abilities to assess critically the full range of
options available to address the common good. The
search for truth has thus been compromised, both within
the leadership team itself and in the aborted possibility of
sincere engagement with the out-group. When diversity
of thought has been stifled within a management team,
stagnation, boredom and a lack of internal resilience set
in. Underlying this experience is often a misunderstand-
ing of consensus that masquerades as a kind of nonhierar-
chic model of managing disagreement and decision
making.

GROUPTHINK:

An Unconscious Effort on the Part
of a Leadership Team (or "In-Group")
to Fortify Itself against Perceived
Threats from "Out-Group" Members

Groupthink is especially serious and should not be underestimated. It is a known fact of group analysis that the membership of any large group reflects and responds to the deficiencies of its leaders. Thus, when diversity of opinion, conflict and serious dialogue find little or no room for expression in the management team, employees will unconsciously respond, mirror or react, ultimately jeopardizing the common good. A high degree of group cohesion is likely to develop when a management team is besieged by the reality of a highly stressful environment, a competitive marketplace, the unpredictability and uncertainty of the future and the imminence of cataclysmic change. Living in a state of intense stress that a highly provocative situational context engenders diminishes self-esteem. Physical and psychic exhaustion combined with feelings of personal depreciation and the ever looming possibility of failing gnaw away at even the most secure leaders. Solace is naturally sought within the in-group itself. Unfortunately, this all too frequently leads to heightened in-group insularity, further separating the leadership group from the possibility of accurately assessing external realities.

To counter the unconscious pull toward groupthink, leadership teams may wish to set in place behaviors as well as strategies for critical evaluation of decisions and actions. For example, those leaders who encourage free expression of ideas, promote vigorous dialogue among proponents of various ideas and voice their own opinions at later points in the discussion are more likely to be able to circumvent groupthink than closed, directive leaders. Directive leaders typically articulate their opinions and preferences early in the discussion and stress the importance of arriving at consensus. This has the effect of prematurely establishing a group norm and discourages deviation from that norm. Subtle pressure on dissenting team members serves to reinforce illusions of unanimity and team invulnerability, all the while diminishing the probability of a successful outcome.

Another strategy that leaders might employ to obviate the intrusion of groupthink is to engage evaluators from outside the management group itself. Before seeking an agreement, outside evaluators may be invited to probe the management team for alternatives and to encourage processes focused on surfacing different ways of addressing a given dilemma. The decision-making base is thus broadened by consultation with employees or persons from different disciplines and areas of expertise. Furthermore, final decisions may be postponed until such time as additional alternatives might seriously be considered. Continually, the uncomfortable question must be asked about too much unanimity. In these times, it is no tribute to the members of a management team to say that they have no conflict or difficulties because they always agree with one another; rather, their efficacy resides in their ability to deal with conflict.

BetaCare's CEO chaired every meeting. She spoke often, with the conviction that her perspective was the most enlightened. Her comments were then endorsed or reinforced by her vice-presidents, leaving the remainder of the staff silent in the face of the strong and united front presented by the senior management team. Overt conflict was clearly at a minimum because few employees dared to take issue with what had been articulated by the power base.

Promoting Efficacious Communal Action

Management teams that manage conflict well and avoid the traps associated with groupthink instill in their organizations the belief that it is, indeed, possible for something important and significant to come from concerted communal action directed toward the greater good. If a company has little sense that it is making a difference as a *group* of valued employees, it will experience organizational anxiety, corporate depression and an intensified fear about a danger-filled future. It also will not attract top-notch people to join it. This was the major difficulty with BetaCare. On the other hand, leaders who work well with conflict and thereby promote the internal unity of the work community model a capacity, through a clear commitment to pursue the future together, to make a difference in the world. They exemplify a certain fearlessness and passion in repeatedly calling the organization to fidelity to its identity in mission. It is a proven fact that, if all else is equal, the organization that is more unified and clear about its identity and mission as well as able to convey an unequivocal valuing of the individuals who comprise it will endure beyond the group that is fragmented. BetaCare was clear about its identity and its mission, but its rigid organizational structure impeded the communication of employee value, worth and dignity. To wager a safe bet, PsiNet is far more likely to endure into the next decade than is BetaCare. In other words, integration and unification contribute to life; individualism and self-interest promote organizational demise.

The desire to flourish cannot be an end in itself. Rather, a company seeks to continue in business because it believes it has something to contribute to the common good of a global society and is successful in its efforts. Spiritlinking leaders want to make a tangible difference in the mission of their organizations as they seek to serve society; they want to see something come of all the hard work. They long for that unimaginable excitement and passion that comes with the knowledge that something important has been achieved as a result of the corporate dreams and visions, the enormous degree of commitment and hard work. When any group lacks the sense of anything much happening from a colossal output of effort, it begins to experience itself as not very worthwhile, not very efficacious. What follows is a series of negative corporate consequences: heightened individualism, attrition of membership, loss of meaning and identity, and corporate malaise.

While many leaders experience a degree of satisfaction in knowing that their companies are addressing those compelling needs identified through various corporate mission statements, they frequently question whether the possibility of corporate magnanimous accomplishment may still be just beyond reach.

Working through Resistance at BetaCare

What was the truth that needed to be told at BetaCare? In other words, what was the mode of the corporate resistance? The first objectively measurable indication that something was wrong was most likely the attrition of excellent staff. While other indications of organizational resistance

> *"The desire to flourish cannot be an end in itself."*

might be intuited by an astute leader, the place to begin the process of working through resistance is with objective data. Naming the reality of what was occurring (that is, the *mode* of the organizational resistance—the loss of key employees) opens the discussion and allows the agency to enter into an examination of what was contributing to the diminishment of corporate morale and feelings of being left without life preservers while drowning in a sea of over-whelming social need. The exploration of the reasons why such attrition might be occurring at this point in the agency's history constitutes the second part of working through resistance (that is, the exploration of the *motive* for this occurring *now*). The motives behind the resistance are unconscious organizational motives, not individual employees' motives for taking a particular action. Often, the most volatile part of the process occurs during the exploration of the motives underlying a resistance to enter with vitality into the future. The CEO and other members of the senior management team must prepare themselves to listen to uncomfortable things that they might prefer not hearing. More than anything, they must refrain from becoming defensive, especially as criticism is inevitably directed toward those in authority.

As soon as leaders become defensive, they have aborted the process of working through resistance. When any group is under stress, its members are far more vulnerable to feeling undervalued. Uncertain about their personal and corporate ability to make a difference, the inevitable tendency is to blame whoever is in a position of authority. Groups hold unconscious fantasies that their leaders will metaphorically "save" or "rescue" the group from demise. Leaders will make everything work out toward the good. Obviously, this is an impossible task for any leader. Nonetheless, the fantasy persists until, at some moment, the group realizes that its leaders are not able to effect this messianic task; then members become angry and disillusioned. It is at this point in the history of the company that frustration is directed toward authority figures.

Unfortunately, no leader or management group can save a company. If the organization is saved, it is only through the considerable efforts of many people. Should leaders become seduced into entertaining some messianic fantasy, they become much more alive to criticism and more easily trapped in defensive maneuvers such as blaming, becoming judgmental or critical of employees, becoming overly irritable or secluding themselves. Conversations with employees, if they occur at all, move away from constructive exploration toward buttressed argumentation, ultimately leading to a stand-off and even deeper entrenchment in the resistance to transformation.

If the senior management at BetaCare were able to engage fruitfully in the process of the exploration of the motives behind the resistance, they would then have been able to engage employees in an examination of the possible consequences for the agency if it continued to lose highly trained personnel. The probing of the *implications* of this trend for the future mission of the organization leads the way for the group to begin anew to develop innovative strategic *action.*

The urgency of these times demands that with new eyes and wonderful imagination we tap into our corporate passion in revisioned effort to address the good that we hold in common. To engage in the deliberate investigation of resistance would have ensured BetaCare's continuing to provide much-needed treatment for the emotionally vulnerable in their catchment area.

Engaging together in this efficacious action on behalf of the common good calls each employee to a deeper expression of personal value and meaning and enables work communities to unleash corporate energy toward the promotion

WORKING WITH RESISTANCE AT BETACARE

The Mode:	*Exemplified by:*	*Intervention:*
OBJECTIVELY, WHAT WAS HAPPENING?	LOSS OF KEY STAFF DIFFICULTY FINDING REPLACEMENT	"We've lost 7 key clinicians in the past 3 months and have not been able to attract others to fill these positions."

The Motive:		
WHY IS THIS HAPPENING NOW?	PRESSURE, STRESS, LACK OF A SENSE OF PLANNING FOR FUTURE, LESS CHANCE FOR PEER SUPPORT AND AFFIRMATION	"Could we take a look together at what may underlie this development?"

The Implications:		
WHAT WILL BE THE CONSEQUENCES FOR THE AGENCY IF THIS CONTINUES?	LOSS OF QUALITY CARE, MORE EMPLOYEE ATTRITION, POSSIBLE AGENCY CLOSURE	"This is a worrisome situation from a number of vantages. If we continue this way, what do you think the likely outcome may be?"

The Action:		
WHAT, IF ANYTHING, WILL THE GROUP DO?	DEVELOP PROCEDURES FOR GREATER TEAM SUPPORT, REVISE REPORTING STRUCTURES, ENGAGE IN STRATEGIC PLANNING EFFORTS TOGETHER	"What might we do together in order to remedy this trend before it destroys us?"

of the well-being of all. To lead on behalf of the common good is as exciting as it is heroic. To stay centered on the ultimate vision of unity; to manage conflict in service of what is true, faithful and just; to stand committed to the unfolding meaning of our identity in mission is the substance of leaders who invite conversion and the linking of spirits and hearts at a time when not to do so is, most likely, to toy with death.

Spiritlinking leaders call their organizations to heroism. They call all who work with them to risk entering into those conflictual conversations that will connect us in trust and in hope to one another. These courageous leaders forge the way into the midst of those difficult dialogues that will bring people into deeper and more respectful relationship with all those who long for a society and a world in which communion in spirit and truth prevail. These are the women and men who invite us to passion and help us to face together the different, the other, the frightening and the unexpected so that we may discover ever more deeply that the good that we hold in common is nothing less than the participation in the mystery of the yet unimagined. These are the courageous, great-hearted ones who help us reach new worlds.

Your Turn....

• Many strategies have been developed in recent years to assist in the effective management of conflict. The success of any method is based on a disciplined adherence to process. Of note is the peculiar tendency of some groups, in the midst of a conflict management session, to sabotage its work by debunking the process in midstream. This frequently represents a form of resistance directed toward protecting the group from the uncomfortable consequences of coming to accord and, therefore, needing to take action that will necessitate change. Most conflict management strategies share the following components:

> • a clear formulation of the problem; that is, What is the content of the disagreement?

- a brainstorming session: an opportunity for each participant to propose, without interruption, possible options;
- an options evaluation session during which the advantages and disadvantages of various alternatives are explored;
- a synthesizing session in which commonalities are identified and participants identify areas that hold greater excitement, creativity and potential for the organization; during this session, new approaches may be developed from the synergy of the group;
- a decision session that determines a course of action and a plan for implementation.

Consider a conflictual issue facing your organization today. Regardless of organizational title, imagine selecting a group comprised of healthy persons with varying perspectives to work on this issue together. Who might they be? What might each bring to the table?

- The more volatile the situation and the higher the stakes, the more important it is to engage the assistance of a facilitator. There are, however, numerous situations that do not call for outside facilitation.

Identify a mildly conflictual issue in your immediate work setting. Using the guidelines delineated in this chapter, attempt to arrive at a resolution.

- Obviously, each time a management team achieves accord on a given decision, it does not mean that they have fallen into groupthink. What is important to evaluate are the team's patterns of decision making and the extent to which people voice differing opinions.

Recall some recent management decisions. What perspective or opinion did you hold? What diverging opinions were expressed by others in the group? At what point in the deliberation did you make known your ideas?

- Altruism increases as persons feel that they are making a difference in society. Similarly, when employees have some sense that belonging to a particular organization provides them with opportunities to join forces with others to make a greater impact on society, there are apt to be higher levels of work satisfaction and less attrition.

How would you describe your personal contribution to making a difference?

How does your company, through the concerted efforts of the employees, contribute to the common good of society?

What might you do to make these insights more tangible to all who work with you?

Chapter 5

FOSTERING COMMUNITY, INTERPRETING METAPHORS

I am reminded of a lengthy discussion I had years ago with a hospitalized patient concerning her fear, actually her terror, of two things: losing her mind and having her home broken into. In the early sessions of the treatment of this very frightened and emotionally fragile woman, she expressed in some detail a metaphor that described her current psychological experience. It went something like this: She was terrified of having her home broken into and of being raped by the intruder; she expressed a need to put more locks on her doors and bars on her windows; when the doorbell rang, she ran into her room and hid. She had a deep sense that she teetered on the edge of losing her grip on reality.

Similarly, once upon a time, there was a very powerful nation that was very frightened of losing its power. The rest of Earth's nations agreed that it was in the best interests of the planet to move toward disarmament. Especially devastating to human beings was the proliferation of land mines, so all the other nations decided to stop producing them. But this very powerful nation could not relinquish its independence and refused to comply with the other countries. Perhaps it, too, stood on the precipice of reality.

Listening to the Metaphor

Metaphor is a window into the heart of human desire and longing. It reveals the human spirit as it fuses our most deeply held beliefs with lived experience. Metaphor expresses the kernel of what has been "forgotten" in the whirlwind of busy lives. It holds the power to break through all that stands in the way of what is true. It stands at the center of the power of the mystic, the artist, the poet and the healer to bring forth profound transformation. It resides in the core of spiritlinking leaders committed to fashioning more compassionate and respectful relationships among those with whom they interact and do business. Because it touches on truth, a metaphor interpreted always provokes change of one sort or another. Consequently, metaphors are usually disturbing, both to the speaker and to the listener. A metaphor disturbs because it cannot be pursued very far without our being led to the very boundaries of what is most sacred. It cannot be grasped at the level of the intellect alone—it is an empathic resonance of the spirit, an expression of what is most true. Like a parable, metaphor uses ordinary language to express the extraordinary truth of what it means to be human.

"Like a parable, metaphor uses ordinary language to express the extraordinary truth of what it means to be human."

What is the meaning of the metaphor used by the hospitalized patient? If we hear her statements simply on the level of the content she shared, we might suggest she get a better security system for her home or encourage her to become more cautious about letting people come to her home because, indeed, the world is a hostile place and she is likely to be taken advantage of if she is not careful. Hearing the metaphor, however, we begin to understand that she is telegraphing a message to her therapist: she is fearful of being intruded upon in treatment; of being asked questions that she does not wish to answer; of being hurt, or perhaps destroyed, through this process of therapy. Also, what might be the meaning of the metaphor in the story of the powerful and self-sufficient nation? Perhaps beneath the bravado resides an equally terrifying fear that the country will ultimately find itself disempowered; that its engagement with other nations may result in more being exacted from it than it believes it can provide; that it may be harmed in the process of becoming increasingly interdependent. In both cases, fear resulted in becoming fortified, defended, armed and isolated.

Fear causes many companies and organizations to engage in corporate behaviors that distance, protect and cause them to threaten one another in much the same way that fear has resulted in personal and national dysfunction. Anxiety masks underlying, basic emotions such as feelings of inadequacy and powerlessness. It is fair to say that these feelings have understandably intensified in most organizations as external structures have become less predictable and more fluid in responding to the pace of change. Ambiguity becomes more prevalent and anxiety concurrently mounts. Lack of a clear vision for the future and rapid reconfigurations of organizational alliances, often accompanied by an inherent loss of individual corporate status, tempt groups to arm themselves, perhaps ever so covertly, against impending crises of diminishment and the loss of what once was. As difficult as it is to let go, spiritlinking leaders know that the seduction of hanging on will lead to organizational demise. Loss always carries with it heightened anxiety. To compensate for that anxiety, some organizations may attempt to cover over their fear by interacting for a time in apparent "peaceful coexistence" with the "competition," all the while becoming cleverly armed, perhaps even subtly armored, against being overtaken by the other. Within the workplace itself, fear may lead coworkers simply to co-exist with one another, waiting in some passive-aggressive way for the other to make a wrong move so that domi-nance can once again be asserted. The greater the feelings of threat, the more the tendency to become defended and defensive and the more intense the resistance to change.

The transformative leader monitors the level of defensive-ness in the organization and deftly works to interpret the metaphor. It is another way of naming what is really going on. Left uninterpreted, defensive interaction leads to the damaging of reality as it worms its way toward the decaying of the work community. In a sobering statement by Archibald MacLeish, "A world ends when its metaphor has died."[6] The spiritlinking leader realizes that entwined in the metaphors of our day is the longing for connection, meaning and belonging. These leaders have the courage to interpret the metaphor. They realize that meaning is wrapped into the heart of the language. They know that businesses and insti-tutions today cannot exist with locks on their knowledge and guards at the gates of collaboration and innovation. They interpret metaphor by risking to tell the truth about what is happening in a world struggling to find meaning and interconnection in a world that longs for community.

The Corporate Community as Metaphor

Community is the deliberate, human expression of such yearning for relationship and purpose. As in other areas of societal life, the corporate world becomes a critical part of the process of building organic, networked bridges among people. Corporate communities offer another opportunity to connect islands of the spirit where commitment to the greater good can flourish. By recognizing the potential of becoming disarmed and interdependent, spiritlinking leaders engage in active planning directed toward cooperation and teamwork. They arduously invest themselves in fashioning a workplace where debate and isolationism are replaced by dialogue and collaboration. They hear the metaphor. At a profound level, they resonate with the truth that to survive as a civilization and as a planet, nations must stop arming themselves; countries must move from isolated nationalism to interdependent sharing of the Earth's resources; and people must deepen in their mutual trust. As organization leaders they are pivotal because they serve as catalysts to build community among those who labor to do good.

COMMUNITY:

The Human Expression

of the Yearning for

Relationship and Purpose

In many ways it is far easier to discuss global issues of disarmament and relinquishing of defense strategies than it is to examine how this might be accomplished in an organization. Individual security and self-protection are deeply cherished values, but at what point do these qualities begin to impinge upon the very life they seek to harbor? At whatever level the leader enters into the interpretation of this century's metaphor to connect and move beyond individualism, that leader will effect change on every other level of this healthily disruptive paradigm. To pay homage to the power of the metaphor, the leader knows that in some mysterious way, building collegial networks among employees and colleagues will impact global struggles to move beyond nationalism and economic greed and self-absorption. Because adamant and unbending institutional arrogance blocks the healing potential of the metaphor, spiritlinking leaders work furiously to dismantle myths of stand-alone enterprises. In so doing, they hold forth the possibility of a world community based on mutual respect, healthy interdependence, and commitment to the good that is held in common.

What Are the

Corporate Metaphors

That Call for
Interpretation Today?

Relationship and Purpose

In order to interpret corporate metaphors, leaders must engage their institutions in reflecting on the ways that the organization may be defending itself against perceived threats. An objective examination of the impact these behaviors may be having on collaborative or networking endeavors leads the group to surmise what could happen in the larger society if this organization were to become more disarmed and disarming in its relationships in the marketplace. Thus, the way is opened to work through resistance to community building.

Resistance to Collaboration

All groups, whether they are social groups, work groups, treatment groups, large organizations or faculties, develop through various phases as they spend time together. In the interest of simplicity, these phases can be described as *inclusion, confrontation* and *collaboration.* An insidious form of organizational resistance to transformative change occurs when groups become fixated at the level of inclusion or confrontation and thus deprive themselves of the perilous yet invigorating opportunity to engage in the collaboration necessary for dreams to be realized. Inclusive phase work groups are characterized by tentativeness. Employees are reluctant to place their ideas on the table because they have a need to be accepted and respected by their peers. The primary focus of employees in the inclusive phase is on themselves, not on the common work effort. Ambivalence about the extent to which an employee wishes to invest himself or herself in the group effort makes it difficult to set corporate goals with any degree of enthusiasm. For this reason, leaders of groups in the inclusive phase may find themselves discouraged by silence and the predominance of behavior-withholding patterns during project meetings. If they do engage in the process at all, people at this stage tend to be superficial and polite with one another, to refrain from any form of contentious interchange and generally to focus conversations on topics that showcase their personal knowledge or expertise.

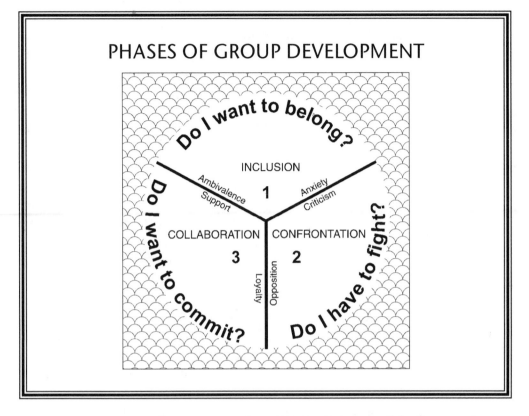

PHASES OF GROUP DEVELOPMENT

Do I want to belong?

Do I want to commit?

Do I have to fight?

INCLUSION
1

Ambivalence
Support

Anxiety
Criticism

COLLABORATION
3

CONFRONTATION
2

Loyalty

Opposition

In some work settings, it is possible for employees never to move beyond this level of interchange. These settings are characterized by a minimum of teamwork, individualized efforts and few, if any, staff meetings. The work environment is the antithesis of community, as it replicates the worst of separatism and heightened individualism. It is basically an aggregate of cubicles that have no doorways into one another's physic or physical space. Leaders who are terror stricken by the thought of organizational change can make certain it will not occur by reinforcing territoriality and nonpermeable work boundaries.

To assist the work group to navigate successfully and as expeditiously as possible through the inclusion phase, spiritlinking leaders recognize the need for individual affirmation and are able to channel individual talent and energy in ways that enhance personal esteem and establish the individual employee as an essential component of the common effort. The capacity to be patient with an inclusion group's hesitation to offer innovative ideas is important because trust is developing invisibly and quite surreptitiously within the group.

More typically, groups are able to move through inclusive issues once colleagues have settled into the task at hand and feel at ease in their own roles within the work group. It is at this point that the initial politeness of the group wears off. At both the conscious and unconscious levels, colleagues begin to focus on issues of power, dominance and control. Attempts to gain allies, enhance status and fortify themselves individually and collectively against authority become evident. Competitive and oppositional behavior patterns are at their peak during the confrontation phase. Negative comments, criticism of coworkers and criticism of management abound. Perhaps the most difficult time for those in leadership roles, the confrontation phase often gives rise to a potentially destructive dynamic of *attackers* and *defenders,* an interplay directed at those who exercise any form of authority. Leaders who understand this dynamic can protect themselves from falling into defensive or vindictive styles of relating with employees. *Attackers* are those members of the work group who repeatedly criticize and devalue persons in authority. *Defenders* are those who protect the continuance of the group task. They do so by countering the negativity of the attackers and disarming the impact of the potential devaluation. It is very difficult for a work group to self-destruct. Forces within the group itself will serve to protect its continuation, even to the extent that the group realizes, at some level, that leadership is necessary for any productive activity. By way of example, consider the following incident:

A substitute teacher took over a sophomore high school geometry class during midquarter. During the first half-hour of her first session with this class, a student raised his hand and announced that the students "detested this class" and did not want to have a substitute teacher. His message was endorsed by three more students. The last student to speak told the instructor that they simply wanted her to leave. The teacher, stunned, left the classroom. While she was standing in the corridor, the principal walked past and asked her what had happened. "They threw me out," she stated with shame. "Oh, don't worry. Just wait here for a few minutes. They'll change their minds," the principal told her. After nearly ten minutes passed, a smiling student presented herself as the class emissary: "We would like to have you come in and teach us. We're sorry. We just were angry that our real teacher isn't here." The fact that the substitute teacher's shock at being asked to leave protected her from becoming defensive with the sophomores was serendipitous. One can surmise that this incident is a classic example of the dynamic described above. Anger at authority was subordinated to the desire of the group to continue its efforts. An entirely different outcome would likely have developed had the teacher refused to leave the classroom and chose, instead, to try to convince the students about her expertise as a geometry teacher. Such defensiveness could have doomed the situation to a quite problematic outcome.

Competition, power issues and the striving for control are means by which colleagues attempt to establish identity as members of a work team. It is a critical time in the formation of a work group. Talented leaders assist the group in maintaining focus on task concerns rather than allowing ad hominem conflicts to flourish, resulting in the pointless sapping of corporate energy. There certainly are instances when teams have become mired in the conflict phase, unable to move forward. Leaders who fail to recognize this trap will watch corporate group efforts evaporate. Similarly, conflict allowed to simmer will only become more noxious. To work effectively with a work group in the confrontation phase, the spiritlinking leader models the capacity to address confrontation proactively with individuals and with the group as a whole. During the inclusion phase, if sufficient efforts have been directed toward confronting individuals with their positive contributions and achievements on behalf of the institution, the groundwork of trust has been established so that more contentious issues can be managed later without causing harm. To engage in negative interchange without such grounding in mutual respect is to limit the chances for such confrontation actually to prepare the way for collaboration.

"...conflict allowed to simmer will only become more noxious."

Becoming paralyzed in inclusion or confrontation serves to protect the group from the consequences of bold collaboration on behalf of the common good. Before examining the characteristics of the collaborative phase of corporate development, an elucidation of the process of working with resistances in groups caught in inclusion or confrontation may be of value. What is assumed, however, is that the astute leader is able accurately to diagnose this phase of the work group's functioning.

RESISTANCE TO COLLABORATION

The Mode (What's happening)

Intervention

INCLUSION

Little disagreement
Silence at staff meetings

Personal affirmation
Work in smaller units
Name what's happening
 "We're a new work group and it'll take
 a little while in order for us to feel free
 to disagree much with one another...."

CONFRONTATION

Negativity, criticism
Subgrouping, cliques
Disgruntlement with authority

Proactive addressing of the issue
Identify what's going on:
 "Our tangling with each other can be
 benefical as long as we can stay focused
 on the issues and not hurt each other...."

The Mode (Why now?)

INCLUSION

Personal insecurity
Ambivalence about investment

"Folks are understandably hesitant to
jump in when we don't really know
each other yet...."

CONFRONTATION

Fears of powerlessness
Fears of loss of control

"As we get closer to facing the
ramifications of the changes we're
designing, we seem more irritable.
How come?"

Implications for the Future

INCLUSION

Conflict avoidance
Avoidance of transformative change

"What will it mean for our work if we
stay this aloof?"

CONFRONTATION

Avoid corporate transformation
Avoid having to let go of familiar

"What will happen with our company
if we continue this cold war with one
another?"

The Action

"What can we do to get ourselves
beyond this?"

The Collaborative Work Community

Spiritlinking leadership results in collaboration on behalf of the mission. If issues related to inclusion and confrontation have been dealt with adequately, the work team will move into a time of collaborative engagement toward the accomplishment of its corporate mission. This does not mean that there will not be times of heated disagreement and conflictual interaction but rather indicates that the establishment of a strong, corporate group identity allows colleagues to value the common good beyond their personal needs to be affirmed, powerful, solely in charge, or assuming the credit for a given project. When a group has entered into true collaboration, colleagues experience mutual support. The NASA Martian expedition team is a fine example of a work group that has entered into collaboration in service of the greater good.

On a practical, observable level, a collaboratively functioning group is notable by its lack of interpersonal defensiveness and judgmental attitudes among colleagues. Persons are free to be themselves. Within an inclusive phase group, it is common for people to refrain from exhibiting highly creative or brilliant ideas for fear of not being seen as "one of the bunch." Persons tend to squelch their individuality and compromise their assertiveness in efforts to be included and accepted; they are not being true to themselves. Likewise, in a group in the midst of confrontation issues, colleagues' apprehensions about being perceived as less authoritative or definitive may lead them to an overly aggressive, interpersonal itchiness as they relate with one another. This may not necessarily be representative of their truest relational style, either. In the collaborative work group, colleagues have grown to trust one another by having dealt with and survived less-comfortable situations that surfaced during the prior developmental phases.

It is at this point in organizational life that community comes alive. It is at this point that businesses hold the promise of making a difference in the global reality as they take steps beyond individualism and alienation, as they dare to interpret the end-of-the-century metaphor that speaks of the need to transcend separatism and competition. The collaborative, corporate community becomes part of the illumination of the living covenant between human beings and the world matrix in which we live and work. The well-being and preservation of creation is dependent upon the commitment of all, no less on corporations than on individuals, to fashion a global community based on principles of interdependence, mutual accountability, a strong mission focus for the good of society and a commitment to mentor future leaders. The authenticity of a truly collaborative corporate community is measured by its embodiment of these values. It is at this point that the spiritlinking leader, in the wondrous mix of humility and pride, takes stock of a job well done.

"Collaborative groups are founded on adult relationships of candor and honesty among colleagues."

When a corporate community manifests interdependence, it exhibits an inherent coherence that enables it to trust its integrity in representing its mission and purpose to the public it serves. It is able to enter into cooperative endeavors without fears of loss of its corporate spirit and mission. Information sharing, networking, nondefensive listening and the ability to articulate independent opinions all give expression to interdependence. Collaborative groups are founded on adult relationships of candor and honesty among colleagues. Such mutual accountability opens the team to rigorous self-evaluation, continual evaluation of differing perspectives and a comfort with delegation and roving authority. Creative cognitive investigation of how to reenvision the corporate mission in

light of unfolding new realities releases enthusiasm as colleagues explore "What if?" ideas far more readily than
"Why should we?" questions. A strong mission focus takes
precedence over maintenance issues. The work group
that has become a community finds energy in creating a
future, not simply in maintaining the present state of
affairs. They have achieved the ability to inspire others to
engage with them in the corporate mission—to exercise
responsibility and to do good on behalf of the society and
world in which they function. Valuing the future contributions that it stands to make, the collaborative corporate
community commits to mentoring the next generation of
spiritlinking leaders. The capacity to author the next generation demands the inner freedom of today's leaders to
relinquish control. This ability is perhaps the final measure of a leader's maturity as he or she believes in the talent of, and entrusts responsibility to, those who are
younger and less experienced.

The Promise of a Corporate Community Realized

The inspirational story of the growth of CHW Health
System, a West Coast not-for-profit health system, provides a moving example of consistent spiritlinking leadership that has guided the company through inevitable
resistances throughout its ten-year life. The health system
was initially formed with the merger of two small health
systems sponsored by Roman Catholic women religious.
The leaders in both congregations knew that the future of
the mission to care for the sick and the poor resided in
combining efforts. To that end, they formed a new entity,
gave up their former corporate names and moved the
headquarters of the new company to a neutral place. Soon

after, another order of women religious approached the new corporation and queried the possibility of becoming a third sponsor of the fledgling system. They had only two hospitals. The deliberations of the board of directors, the original two sponsoring groups and the management team resulted in the third sponsor being incorporated into the system. What was remarkable, however, was not that the third sponsor had been approved to join, but that the newest group, bringing far fewer brick-and-mortar assets, would nonetheless share equally in the governance of the entire system. Such a decision was based not on hard-nosed rationality but on the vision that the corporation would be better positioned to realize its mission and express its values if the third sponsor were coequal. From the earliest days of the formation of the cosponsored system, the foundational values of justice, mercy and care for the poor have inherently guided the astute and markedly fearless management team. Additional risky decisions were made by management and governance as the system invested its assets in a socially responsible investment portfolio and withdrew holdings from companies whose practices violated the promotion of a healthy global community.

As the corporation grew, other health systems and freestanding institutions sought to join. Careful examination of the motivation and cultures of would-be cosponsors became a critical part of the decision-making process. While other value-driven entities became part of the system, some seemingly lucrative mergers and acquisitions were turned down because management and governance would not jeopardize the founding mission. They were unwilling to place at risk the corporate soul and spirit.

The system would not have achieved this degree of mission accomplishment had not its leadership been consistently exemplary. The first CEO and senior management team, along with the founding board of directors of the newly merged system, possessed the founding wisdom, courage and inner authority needed to bring a new model of sponsorship and a different kind of entity into existence. When the time was right, the founding CEO retired, knowing that something extraordinary had been brought to birth under his watch. While the succeeding CEO chosen by the board brought different gifts to the company, a deeply rooted belief in the mission of the system was palpable in this leader. Of particular tribute to him was the fact that none of the founding senior management team left during this transition. A clear commitment to collaboration, team management and subsidiarity has accounted, in large part, for the retention of superb leaders within the corporate management team, as well as throughout regional divisions. Firmly grounded in their sense of authority and committed to community building and participative decision making at every level, few leaders within the system have had a need to be center stage. Typically, leaders who have sought such notoriety have not adjusted to the corporate culture and have moved on.

In speaking with employees in various positions throughout the system, one is struck by the sense of corporate pride individuals hold as they witness the mission take expression in compassionate action on behalf of the needy in their communities. At this point in its history, this health system is an example of a powerfully collaborative organization that continues to manage conflict and resistance sufficiently to enable it to intensify its communal efforts. As a community of 30,000 employees, it serves as a change agent and embodiment of a new metaphor. Inevitably, it will face serious challenges as the health care industry contends with mounting political, economic and social stresses. If the system's passion for its mission can be sustained and deepened through innovative community formation, it will continue to promote healing in those arenas it touches. The system will have an impact on the environment, just as the environment shapes the system.

Those corporations and institutions that enter the next century with vibrancy will have embraced their mission with such commitment and passion that they are willing to enter into the uncomfortable places of risky decision making based on fidelity to their mission and values. They are willing to live with inevitable friction and tension, as these characterize any vibrant organization. To ignore or shirk from confrontation, to stand alone in tentative self-sufficiency, will result in cultural co-optation and ultimate diminishment.

CHW and organizations like it act contrary to the pull toward separatism, aggression and exploitation; they provide a window into a healing metaphor. They help the world reclaim its soul. This is not about organizational arrogance or puffed-up self-importance; it is about commitment and values and an unflinching determination to take action on behalf of a good that is much larger than any one person, any one organization, any single industry. It is about the commitment to search continually for new insights and yet unrevealed meanings of collaboration and community in the midst of turbulent times.

Your Turn....

What are the principal areas of struggle for your company today? How do these target problems affect the formation of community in the global, corporate and intraorganizational arenas?

- These areas of struggle can serve as blocks to the transformation of your organization if they remain unaddressed. Leaders bear the responsibility to catalyze their organizations to address issues. They do not bear the responsibility to "fix" the problems themselves. The manner in which problems will be successfully managed, however, depends upon an accurate assessment of the phase of group development.
- While it would be a wonderfully tidy construct, no organization or work group—beyond its initial founding moments—is totally immersed in inclusion, confrontation or collaboration dynamics. Rather, it is more realistic to find a prevailing set of issues at work that typify a stronger foothold in one or the other stages of group formation and development. Within your management team, for example, you may find yourselves primarily dealing with issues related to collaboration but struggling with power, dominance and control issues from time to time. Consider some of the characteristics of each phase of group development:

Inclusive Phase Behaviors:

- Politeness, caution
- Superficial accord, few disagreements
- Conflict avoidance
- Formality
- Reliance on authority figures

Confrontation Phase Behaviors:

- Competition within work group
- Subgrouping, coalition building
- Covert strategizing
- Territoriality
- Negativity, criticism
- Preoccupation with process rather than task accomplishment
- Persistent irritation with authority figures

Collaborative Phase Behaviors:

- Cooperative task engagement
- Subordination of personal agenda to corporate agenda
- Peer adult relationship with authority figures
- Enjoyment in common project
- Willingness to "go the extra mile"

- Every group likes to think of itself as functioning collaboratively. If the group has not addressed confrontation issues, however, it is impossible for it to engage in true collaboration. It is also impossible for such a group to move from inclusion to collaboration. Typically, when groups suggest that this is what has occurred, they are simply avoiding conflict.

Consider your management team's functioning at this point in time. What phase of team functioning predominates? What are some indicators of remnants of the other two phases?

_____

_____

- Those "remnants" become your targets for working through resistance. As you address these resistant behaviors with the team, it is important to remind yourself and the group that every group moving toward transformative change will find itself intensifying unconscious resistant behaviors. Groups are poised to engage in courageous action toward transformation when they are operating collaboratively, but collaboration is possible only after the group has become comfortable with confrontation.

- **Formulate how you might *name* those impeding behaviors for the team:**

_____

_____

• Specify how you might engage the team in an exploration of the *motives* for the behaviors at this time:

_____

_____

• Reflect upon how you might open the conversation to explore *implications* for your company's mission, should the behavior persist:

_____

_____

Chapter 6

PROVIDING HEALTHY LEADERSHIP

Do you remember, when you were small, knowing a wonderful older kid you just idolized and wanted to be like? Well, when Nini Riordan was ten and I was seven, I was utterly convinced that Nini was the most fantastic little girl I had ever met. She was older than most of the kids on the block, but she would play with us nonetheless, so we all thought she was terrific. She would regularly round us up to do wonderful things. She'd get Lizzy Lewin and Scrap and Mudball Benton and Ritty Salzberg and Katie McKee and me organized into grand games of kick-the-can or timed contests to see who could collect the most locusts. She was particularly adept at enticing Mudball to pick up the locusts that we'd locate in the bushes. Mudball would pick them up gently by their wings and carefully put them in our milk bottles, which we would then lovingly carry home as presents for our mothers. One day, in a particularly daring act of cementing our circle of friends, Nini showed us how to make a magic potion out of milk, ground worms and dandelion leaves. Dabbing a bit on each of our wrists, we knew we would all be sealed as friends forever. Nini would also sometimes lead us in "church." It didn't matter to any of us that Lizzy and Ritty were Jewish and that Scrap and Mudball were Protestants. Nini would teach us some pig latin and we'd devoutly receive Necco wafers on our tongues. The greatest thing was, Nini always treated us as if we were ten years old, too. Nini had a beautiful turquoise dress with big white, fluffy clouds painted all along the border and pink watercolor flowers on the top. I thought it was positively the most beautiful dress in the whole world. One day, when were assembled at Nini's house to play, Nini came downstairs with her beautiful dress in her arms. It was ironed and neatly folded. "Here, this is for you," she said. "I'm getting too tall for it. Besides, I like you!" I wore and wore that dress until one day I, too, got too tall.

Leadership is about building relationships, about unifying a community of colleagues, about believing in the value and worth of each person, about serving and teaching and, when the time comes, about entrusting the next generation with what has been learned. Nini was a wonderful "community organizer" and, perhaps one day, would become a spiritlinking leader. Just as excellent leaders are able to work through resistances that serve to fracture corporate unity in the service of the organizational mission, poor leaders can, themselves, become blocks to the possibility of a solid future because they fail to represent the truth. Four types of these "pseudoleaders" are especially dangerous and resistant forces in any organization: the Unrecovering Addict, the Narcissistic Personality, the As-If Leader and the Alexithymic Talking Head. While the descriptions that follow are, admittedly, caricatures, even the best leaders may discover remnants of these features in themselves when they face intense pressure and internal stress. What is essential is the recognition of these symptoms and expeditious treatment.

The Unrecovering Addict

Misdirected efforts to assume control over situations that cannot be controlled can result in a plethora of compulsive and addictive behaviors. The addicted person binds the anxiety generated from feeling out of control by engaging in repetitive, frequently destructive and sometimes life-threatening behaviors. In the work setting, these leaders often present themselves as intermittently ingratiating and irritable.

Jim was a middle-aged, middle manager who in many ways characterized what it means to be a sensitive human being caught in the confusion of a business world in the throes of cataclysmic transformation. Reengineering, right-sizing and the likelihood of merger preyed daily on his sense of security. Not unsurprisingly, those who are among the most sensitive and the most alive to the world around them are frequently those at greatest risk of falling victim to addictive behaviors and emotional distress. Jim's presenting problem was something rather unusual—not an ordinary case of addiction or marital problems or depression. He had become addicted to peanut-butter-and-jelly sandwiches. Each day he would have his wife cut up eight "pb&j's," each sandwich cut into twenty-four bite-sized pieces that he would carefully pack into his briefcase and then set off for work. In six months' time he had bulked up his 5′7″ frame from 150 pounds to a walloping 210 pounds. His wife was becoming increasingly infuriated. His coworkers were talking about him behind his back. He had failed to receive a promotion because he was unable to carry his sandwiches into the interview session with the company CEO and, as a consequence, became so anxious and demonstrated such personal insecurity that he was unable to engage effectively in the conversation. Deprived of the solace, comfort and the compulsive binding activity that the pb&j's pretended to offer, Jim was a wreck. By the time he sought help, his marriage was in jeopardy, he had failed for the third time to receive a promotion and he was in imminent danger of losing his job. He felt alienated, frightened, compulsively preoccupied and, most sadly of all, he felt certain he was a profound failure.

Jim was a pathetically strained and agonized person, a casualty of the times, who embodied the repercussions of a culture in which competition and dehumanization have run rampant and in which human beings have struggled to find comfort in illusions of dependency. Whether it be alcohol, drugs, work, peanut-butter-and-jelly sandwiches— or any other of a raft of addictive behaviors—such dependencies masquerade as deleterious inoculations against a scarred culture. They momentarily trick the victim into feeling comforted in the midst of massive change. At the same time, they increasingly and insidiously deprive the person of the very thing needed to promote healing: strong, mutual relationships. Something was missing in Jim's personal and professional life. He lacked a sense of colleagueship. His relationship with his wife had become one of a parent and a child, with the parent sending the child off to work with his brown sack of peanut butter sandwiches. Computer technology and new business practices were intimidating, and he felt overwhelmed, inferior, anxious and increasingly out of control as programs and machines were moving in to take over his work. He increasingly felt like an ignorant child in a grown-up world. Dependency had taken the place of partnership. Community was missing in every aspect of his life.

Left unaddressed, addictive behavior in a person in a leadership role will create especially serious impediments for any group—whether that be in a family system or in an organization—because such behavior is founded upon the falsehood that change can be contained and transformation can be halted. Its consequence is more-profound isolation as human connections become more and more damaged. The untruth in the assumption that change can be avoided is reinforced by the fantasy that codependent and dependent relationships can replace the gratification felt in a community of partners. Dependency and denial characterize institutions led by unrecovering addicts. As a result, the obviation of the process of networking and collaboration becomes a serious manifestation of destructive organizational resistance.

The Narcissist as Leader

Narcissists can wend their way to leadership positions because of their projection of power, control and self-assurance. A facade of social polish initially assists these leaders to be well received by colleagues and employees. They possess a charismatic ability to lure others into following them. They tend to present themselves quite positively to search committees and are adept at cajoling persons into liking them. Typically, at the start, these leaders are quite popular and generate considerable organizational excitement as they enter into positions of responsibility. Often seen as "saviors" in struggling organizations, they assume unwavering control. The organizational enthusiasm is short-lived, however, as persons soon intuitively sense that something is lacking. Grandiosity and suspiciousness in the narcissistic leader begin to give rise to impulsive decision making and random disregard of organizational processes. Believing that they alone possess the truth and that others simply exist to mirror their need to receive continued adulation, they engage in subtle tactics of devaluation of any employees who do not serve this purpose. Arrogance and self-righteousness begin to seep through the veneer of social propriety and the inclusive phase of their tenure comes to a close. Any challenge to the decisions of narcissistic leaders is met with vengeance, overt hostility, and autocratic and vindictive requital. Splitting the work group into persons who are on the side of the narcissistic leader and those who are against the leader is a classic form of resistance seen in an organization led by a narcissist. Actually, the splitting of the resistance itself is often the clearest diagnostic determinant of this pathological leader.

John was a high-profile person in the civic community. He was frequently interviewed by media because of his noteworthy action on behalf of the homeless; he had also received numerous commendations by various philanthropic groups for his speaking and writing on behalf of the abandoned. The entire town took pride in John because he was engaged in such charitable work and, ostensibly, represented its most cherished values. He was named to head a prestigious, regional blue-ribbon committee to investigate remedies addressing the problems of the poor and abandoned in the state. Believing he would be best able to garner the support of large funding sources, civic leaders entrusted him with the task of leading this important group. What actually ensued was disastrous. Of ten highly talented and committed community leaders who had been chosen to work with John, only two survived beyond the first four months of meetings. Through interviews with those who left the committee, the following experiences were noted:

· While John clearly possessed creative ideas about how to go about enlisting community financial support, committee members felt their ideas frequently were facilely dismissed or sometimes even ridiculed.

- When two members disagreed with the approach John was advocating because they were concerned about ethical ramifications, they were told that perhaps it would be in their best interests to resign.
- Each time a committee member had been approached by the press in his or her own civic community and asked to comment on the progress of the project, John became enraged and indicated that he alone was to speak on behalf of the effort. This led to feelings of dismissal and to an overall sense of not being trusted on the part of these competent women and men.
- When John himself was speaking publicly about the efforts of the group, he exaggerated his own efforts to the extent that committee members felt he was actually dissimulating. They feared that the public's financial support would be built on untruths.
- In interaction with local politicians, he never acknowledged the work of anyone other than himself.
- The two persons who remained on the committee sided with John in degrading the other committee members. This led to insurmountable tension in the group because John's own inner conflicts were now being externalized and acted out in the committee.

By far the most dangerous pathology in a leader, narcissism disrupts the healthy exercise of authority and accountability in an organization. Narcissists are not team people. They find it difficult, if not impossible, to share the stage with anyone. While their intentions may be good, their inability to manage their need for absolute attention leads to the downfall of every effort in which they become engaged. In the situation with John, none of those who worked with him was dependent upon him for his or her livelihood. They were simply able to withdraw from the committee. Unfortunately, this is not often the case in most corporations that find themselves being led by a narcissist.

Groups seldom recognize the source of organizational difficulty until it has reached critical proportions. Because of the narcissist's capacity to externalize blame in credible ways, coworkers are slow to identify the negative organizational pull with the personality of the leader. By the time the source of the problem has been accurately targeted, employees have often been so manipulated and intimidated that they lack the stamina to take any action directed toward confronting the leader. The hope is that the narcissist will experience sufficient psychic pain, perhaps stemming from conflicts in public arenas, that lead to some tarnishing of their image and that some external intervention will ensue in the face of their rage. Another possibility is that colleagues and employees can coalesce sufficiently to call for an outside consultant to be engaged to analyze and assist in remedying the faltering situation. This, at best, is a tenuous undertaking. Narcissists lack the capacity for honest self-examination and are too rigidly defended to hear feedback. When confronted, they typically terminate their position—actually the best of all outcomes because their continuation with the organization will serve only to entrench it in deadening resistance to transformation. Narcissists do not fundamentally change.

The "As-If" Leader in the Empty Suit

As-if leaders have learned how to enact and how to behave in that role, but the substance of personal identity and inner authority is lacking. Because they have a well-developed talent for mimicry, they find themselves from time to time in positions of leadership. Superficially playing the role of what they believe is that of a leader, they are in a state of continued apprehension that their deceit will be discovered. Most significantly, these leaders have a strong need to be liked by others. In fact, their insatiable need to be appreciated by employees makes it extremely difficult for them to make hard decisions that could result in negative responses. These poor leaders exhibit a need to be liked that outweighs their need to accomplish the transformative task. In their desperate need to be liked, these leaders may assume the role of the all-nurturing, overly solicitous parent who seeks to satisfy all employees' needs for gratification. The employees' delusion is that the leader understands them and will take care of them. If left in the position for very long, these leaders will attract dependent, needy workers whose subjective discomfort is as great or greater than that of the leader.

While every leader harbors moments of self-doubt and worries, from time to time, about being able to accomplish successfully the daunting tasks at hand, the as-if leader's fundamental neediness is what distinguishes him or her from this ordinary level of concern in healthy leaders. Furthermore, as-if leaders' deep-seated feelings about being inauthentic and inadequate make it difficult for them to make any significant goal-directed decisions. Procrastination becomes the hallmark of their style and the organizations they lead become transfixed in paralysis. It goes without saying that these leaders' posturings have grave consequences for organizations seeking to engage in transformative change.

The advantage that as-if leaders have over narcissists is that their personal level of anxiety and inner anguish frequently leads them to seek professional consultation. Their assumption of leadership roles is likely a marked disservice to them because it heightens intrapsychic anxiety to such an extent that they inflict harm on themselves as well as on the organizations they attempt to lead. Consultation often results in their obtaining positions in which they are not solely responsible for the corporate outcome. Should an organization leave in place an as-if leader, it passively colludes in resistance. It has effectively made it impossible for necessary change to proceed.

The Talking Head as Leader

Talking-head leaders are alexithymic; that is, they function from a fundamental base of denying emotion. Impervious to their own feelings as well as to the sentiments of others, they relate to their coworkers from a stance of depersonalized indifference. These roboticized leaders are ineffective because they are affectively disconnected from others and are regularly experienced as aloof and distant. Their primary defenses are intellectualization and rationalization. Decisions are made based on reason alone. Seldom do they take risks. Cool, thorough, plodding rationality governs their actions. Organizations run by talking heads are not particularly exciting or innovative places because these companies typically lack passion. They specialize in maintenance functions and are expert in keeping firm control. Classic organizational resistances of legalism and rigidity characterize groups led by talking heads.

When the organization moves into the confrontation phase and anger begins to surface in the work group, these leaders feel overwhelmed. Strong emotion is incomprehensible, and they become stymied when logic will not suffice to quell the conflict. It is actually this occurrence that holds some hope for the talking head because he or she is then likely to seek consultation. Again, left unaddressed, this type of dysfunctionality in a leader will block transformation.

The unrecovering addict, the narcissist, the as-if leader and the talking head do damage to organizations of all kinds. These pseudoleaders only appear to possess basic leadership competencies. Additionally, they lack reflective depth and psychological balance. Not only are they unable to enter into the process of spiritlinking, but they also risk destroying whatever community networking may be developing through informal leadership channels.

The Spiritlinking Leader

Leaders for the future must be excellent leaders committed to building networks of relationships through which visions can be approached. These spiritlinking leaders are mentors who are no strangers to risk taking, who, from the depths of their own commitment to the greater good, work deliberately and directly at establishing processes that liberate the collective spirit of their organizations and place that energy at the service of the global community. Grounded in reflective evaluation, these are trusting and trustworthy people who inspire commitment to the vision of a more unified world. They are not afraid to identify and work through resistances at work in themselves and in their organizations, nor are they apprehensive about developing strategies and taking bold actions that will lead to profound institutional conversion and transformation. These are the leaders who will dare to lead to places where others may be afraid to go on their own.

In a comprehensive research study on leadership, David Nygren and Miriam Ukeritis[7] found that outstanding leaders possess basic competencies of information gathering, administrative adeptness and efficiency; the cognitive abilities of conceptualization and analytical thinking; and a strong sense of mission. In addition, these leaders also possess a profound awareness of the sacredness of life, which enables them to discern and speak to the meaning of what is happening in a changing world. They have a passion for making things better and to making things happen. They consistently focus on strategy over maintenance, on where the institution desires to go and how it will get there, rather than on sustaining the everyday functioning of the status quo. Objective and truthful about what is going on, they are able to subordinate their need to be liked and affirmed to the need to accomplish an important task. They are responsive to signs of resistance and move forward to address resistances as a common part of their professional obligations.

As dysfunctional leaders foster paranoid, depressed and conflicted organizations, the spiritlinking leader's success is predicated on reflective depth and psychological equilibrium. Such qualities enable these leaders to build networks of relationships that combine and capitalize on the leadership talents of each member in the organization. In large part, such effective leadership contributed to the success of the CHW Health System. Its organizational relationships reflect unity and grace and thus inspire the entire employee community to be agents of change for the good of the global community.

Spiritlinking leadership forms the basis of the effective exercise of participative authority and the formation of strategic teams that spend as much time in reflective examination of contemporary interpretations of the mission as they do in the hard work of achieving it. Participative authority is not synonymous with democracy. Having influence and being listened to, being valued and supported, and sharing deeply held values is not the same as having a vote. Majority rule or absolute consensual agreement are not necessarily decision-making styles that will break open the future any more than will authoritarian or dictatorial modes. Too often, consensus has resulted in cautious, untimely and unimaginative action that arises more from what has been familiar than from the eruption of synergistic surprise. Spiritlinking leaders work to develop modified consensual strategies that leave the door open for the unexpected.

Because spiritlinking leaders are secure in themselves, arbitrariness, fear, secrecy and defensiveness find little room in their organizations. As they are secure and emotion-

"Spiritlinking leaders work to develop modified consensual strategies that leave the door open for the unexpected."

ally healthy, their organizations grow in wholeness and security. Unlike dysfunctional leaders, who are preoccupied with how they, along with their companies, will weather the rough times ahead, spiritlinking leaders convey passion and excitement as they call their organizations to explore transformative alternatives.

Staying Healthy

It is no secret that stress takes a marked toll on persons who are sensitive to the world around them today and who are committed to taking transformative action. The very impact of rapid change and the disruption it necessarily creates causes even the most resilient human being to feel disconcerted, disconnected and anxious sometimes. A plethora of self-help books addresses the topic of stress management, but only a few espousing supportive strategies for spiritlinking leaders in their efforts to promote healthy organizations are of note.

Perhaps more than any other factor, strong relational ties characterized by acceptance, flexibility and humor offset the toll taken by work overload and the tendency to hold unrealistic self-expectations. Isolation diminishes leader effectiveness and leads to misperceptions of the corporate reality. Spiritlinking leaders typically hold themselves to high standards. They have a need to see themselves and their organizations accomplish what they have set out to do. Given these expectations, friendships and healthy intimate relationships support a continued realistic appraisal of what is actually possible and reasonable for themselves personally and for their organizations to undertake within a given frame of time. Spending time and energy on strategic issues, planning and multidimensional processing of alternatives taps into the leader's creativity while an overinvestment of time spent on maintenance issues and micromanaging spawns heightened levels of frustration. Leaders who lack such relational support and who are trapped in energy-depleting communication inefficiency are at risk for depression and demoralization. When depression begins to take grip, leaders lose a sense of objectivity. Personalizing of conflicts, defensive tactics and oversensitivity to criticism are indicators that the leader is at risk. Difficulties in concentration and problems with sleep and eating are additional indicators that the leader needs outside consultation.

In this day and age it is an accepted given that taking time for physical care and rejuvenation is a proven antidote for high stress levels. Similarly, commitment to periods of meditative reflection, introspection and solitude offset affective depletion because they offer opportunities for highly charged leaders to recapture meaning and refocus vision.

Spiritlinking leaders maintain emotional and physical well-being by staying true to visionary direction, to strategic goals, to action directed toward goal achievement, to a high degree of team interaction and to an inner spirituality that provides clarity of purpose. Their need to work toward the accomplishment of the corporate mission supersedes their need to be liked. Thus, they are able to achieve collective organizational outcomes that serve the common good and strengthen the global community.

Your Turn....

• Most people today are highly aware of what they ought to be doing to stay healthy. Many of us in high stress positions, however, have serious difficulties trying to maintain healthy balance in our personal and professional lives. Spiritlinking requires the efforts of well-integrated leaders. To ensure the continuance of effective leadership, it is helpful from time to time to "take inventory."

PHYSICALLY—

Are you aware of any unhealthy practices with respect to your eating? drinking? sleeping? exercising? If so, name the behaviors:

_____

_____

SPIRITUALLY—

Do you take time out for reflection, meditation, solitude or silence on a consistent basis? If not, what is preventing you?

_____

_____

EMOTIONALLY—

As you think back over the past few weeks, identify feelings that seem to have predominated. Anxiety? Irritation? Excitement? Depression? Sadness? Enthusiasm? Inability to focus? Hurt? Exasperation? Others?

_____

_____

RELATIONALLY—

A former CEO of a large Canadian corporation is said to have offered the following advice to an up-and-coming executive: "I always make a point of eating supper with my family at least four or five times a week, regardless of what my schedule looks like." Quality time with loved ones and friends inoculates against personal depletion.

During the past week, when have you felt appreciated, loved by spouse, family, friends? Identify some specific instances when you have expressed support, love and affection toward them.

- Often, so-called negative feelings combine with physical, spiritual and relational depletion to form the colloquial phenomenon of "burnout." Resistance to self-care sets the stage for this destructive state to take hold. One means of inoculating yourself against burnout is to work through your own resistances to taking care of yourself. Using the material above, you have likely identified some behaviors that are impeding you in your ability to exercise spiritlinking leadership.
- Take some time out to work through the process of resistance using the four-step schema:

Identify the mode of the potentially destructive behavior:

Hypothesize about some of the reasons that this behavior might be taking a stronger hold on you now (that is, the previously unconscious motive behind the behavior):

Explore the implications for your personal and professional life if this behavior continues:

Finally, ask yourself what you are willing to do to move beyond its unhealthy hold on you:

_____

_____

Chapter 7

PUTTING IT ALL TOGETHER

"Imagine a farmer going out to sow some seed. As he sowed, some seeds fell on the edge of the path and were trampled on, and the birds of the air ate them up. Some others fell on patches of rock where they found little soil, and when they came up they withered away because they had no moisture. Some other seeds fell among thorns and the thorns grew with them and choked them. And some seed fell into rich ground and they grew and produced an enormous crop.

Listen, anyone who has ears to hear!"

Matthew 13:4–9

Leaders who have become adept at spiritlinking have ears to hear. They have mastered the ability to ground themselves. Rooted and centered, these vibrant people have learned to make contact with and stay connected to their life-source along rocky, thorn-choked paths fraught with oftentimes exhausting situations. They know how to bend in grace and take well-grounded, purposeful action in the face of the winds of resistance. They captivate others to join them in creative solidarity as they keep watch on a still distant and mysterious horizon. These are the selfless, energetic women and men who remain flexible and sufficiently confident to assume the task of superb leadership. They will yield sustenance for a transforming world. In touch with their souls, with their own spirit, they daily uncover and share new lifeforms within and around them. They have grasped the fundamental role of excellent leadership: to promote the unity and the life of the groups they serve. In so doing, they are the messengers who will advance global communion.

As they tap into their own spirit, these leaders invite the mythic members of a postmodern tribe to gather in a circle of healing where a world aching from soul-loss can be called to transformation. Committed to the ongoing transformation of themselves and their institutions, they exude characteristics that free energy and creativity—liberate spirit—in order to overcome the resistances impeding the realization of planetary unity. Personal integration affords them the enviable opportunity to sink deep roots into rich soil, between thorny moments and along sometimes misguided paths.

Linking

As each organization contends with its particular struggles to enter the future with vitality and purpose, there are common themes apparent in any self-aware group. Blocks to transformative change coalesce around issues related to *lack of organizational clarity about identity and mission; conflict mismanagement and the misuse of power and authority; fears of collaboration, interdependence and community building; and the dis-ease of leadership, leader pathology and exhaustion.* These common motifs are countered by "spiritlinks" and, as discussed previously, are addressed through the successful management of resistances.

Mission-driven vision, conflict management, community and inner authority—all predictably suffused with an energetic and *agitated resistance*—become the spiritlinks that usher in transformation. To move forward into the uncertain maelstrom of the decades ahead, to bridge disunity through an unfaltering commitment to the promotion of community in all spheres of personal and corporate life, supplies the impetus for the spiritlinking leader. A deep respect for the sacred, along with an unswerving courage to manage conflict, provides the context for leaders to address resistance to global conversion. There is no viable option for the leader who chooses to engage in this potentially redemptive act but to confront the terror of being upset and to embrace the humility of making mistakes.

This is sacred time. This is a time for grounding. It is a time for those who have the ears to hear. To be entrusted with leadership today inspires a profoundly vibrant belief in a faithful, self-organizing spirit at work in our world. That life-force will usher in the new if we clear the way and refuse to stifle its emergence. Spiritlinking thus affords the awesome opportunity to foster the spirit of community that a broken world so desperately craves. The spiritlinking leader serves as a linkage for the hope and the promise that are embedded in the hearts and spirits of every being, of every living organization. They participate in and promote global healing as they choose collaboration and cooperation over competition and as they engage in interdisciplinary exchange that respects the dignity, expertise and experience of each person. Capitalizing on the challenge of working with resistance, they celebrate the synergy that unfolds out of the agar of vastly divergent opinions as new configurations move their organizations toward greater coherence and renewed efficacy. These creative and committed leaders mentor attentive listening as they stay attuned to the stirrings of their own hearts,

> *"Spiritlinking... affords the awesome opportunity to foster the spirit of community that a broken world so desperately craves."*

their sacred space where they have learned the freedom of personal transparency and nondefensiveness.

Spiritlinking leaders have faith in the power of the human connection to sustain hope in the midst of creative chaos. They trust in the yearning resident in the soul as it stretches toward deeper meaning and purpose. These are the truth tellers who care enough about the future of creation to bear the consequences of their insights. Truth telling addresses the modes of resistance to change. In this time of teetering on the verge of global transformation, the commitment to tell the truth about what is happening is the first act in working through the resistance to community, to corporate conversion and, ultimately, to global transformation.

Their capacity for interdependence bespeaks their comfort in trusting the collective wisdom of the group. Leaving behind the enticement of individualism, these talented leaders have entered the heart of community building and, in so doing, have assumed a prominent position in effecting profound change in their organizations as well as in the environment in which their companies exist. Interdependent leaders relate without exaggerated egotism as they express their insights as part of an unfolding truth.

Grounding

Inner authority, reverence and wisdom provide a base for managing conflict and being able to withstand the high levels of frustration felt as firm, rich ground is sought. Inner authority resides in the heart of the leader who is at home in the midst of conflict and who is rooted in sufficient self-confidence to manage complex situations without inordinate anxiety. The image of the spiritlinking leader as one who is *grounded* is apt in a world where the very ground—our land, the foundations of our existence and our sustenance—is endangered, in a world in which persons' connections with their spirits, with the very *ground of their being,* become a deeply valued pursuit. Grounded people withstand and make creative use of the full range of turbulent emotions. Centered, resilient and flexible, they are not easily pushed over. Grounded leaders are in reverent touch with the bedrock of their own existence and are firmly connected to the ground on which they journey.

As grounded leaders are in contact with themselves and with their surrounding communities, they receive insight and energy from the life around them. Similarly, grounded organizations interact in a dynamic release of energy that erupts as they take action toward establishing a healthier and more compassionate global future. They realize that we share common ground.

Moving beyond the dualistic thinking that separates who one *is* from what one *does,* the spiritlinking leader exudes an inner peace and energy that issues from an inherent integration of the self with lifework. These leaders' *identity,* or sense of self in the world and in relation to others, is enhanced because of finding personal meaning in *service of the mission.* A sense of grounding, of continuity, of coherence between the self and lifework is exemplified in the lives of these leaders because they have opened themselves to the often uncomfortable but profoundly enriching experience of ongoing inner transformation and conversion. These are the leaders who have been able to shed their own character armoring. For them, spirit is not kept encased. They have freed themselves of any "tomb for the spirit"[8]; as they have allowed themselves to surrender to greater life and have entered more profoundly into the process of transformation.

Somewhat ironically, they have discovered that it is in

the very act of letting themselves delve deep into the core of unexplored creativity that they tap into the genuine sadness of letting go of the familiar past. Spiritlinking leaders are aware of the grief that comes from the long process of sinking roots into unfamiliar soil, of going into the depths, of tenuously probing the fertile richness of the darkness. Fear is dispelled and grounding occurs as deep breaths are taken in and released, as the flow of energy is felt throughout one's being, as balance is again restored.

At its very essence, the act of spiritlinking beckons to the ground of a transformative world community. It operates across all facets of societal and corporate life as it persists in its commitment to address inevitable resistances that impede the realization of a just, global interdependence. It requires grounded leaders who, in freedom and creativity, pledge themselves to facilitate the working through of those impediments staving off the promotion of global unity. Capable of seeing the incontrovertible data supporting the progressive destruction and exploitation of resources, these extraordinary leaders point the way toward identifying the resistances we face relative to ensuring a viable planetary future.

Spiritlinking has failed if it ignores the importance of the act of *grounding* in relation to the environmental agenda today. Grounded in internal integrity, rooted in the community, connected and interactive, spiritlinking leaders know that their organizations are situated in the midst of a fragile global ecosystem. Their companies and institutions are rooted on this land, on this ground, and they are obligated to protect that ground as it continues to offer sustenance to all that walk upon it. It remains curious that denial about the seriousness of the environmental crisis continues to operate so insidiously in many institutions today. Jokes directed toward minimizing the extent and gravity of the situation all too often find curious

"At its very essence, the act of spiritlinking beckons to the ground of a transformative world community."

places at board tables and finance meetings. Clearly, the danger of this manifestation of resistant denial cannot be overstated. Any organization today that remains impervious to its impact on the environment and resistant to taking action toward global healing is acting in psychopathic exploitation. As it depletes energy from others, it enters into a stance of alienation and ultimately nudges itself toward death. Cultural historian Thomas Berry so crisply stated well over a decade ago, "An exhausted planet is an exhausted economy."[9] Without doubt, those who serve in leadership positions in developed countries bear a particular moral weight to risk spiritlinking through this extraordinarily dangerous form of denial.

Illuminating Energy

Spiritlinking leaders are giants whose vision and passion illuminate the way for institutions, businesses, corporations, faith communities and nations to build bridges toward a sustainable future. As starlight's emitted energy is attracted toward solid mass, as the processes of *sending forth* and *drawing toward* form a dancing interplay in the cosmos, spiritlinking leaders spark that intrinsic connection between mission and collaboration, between goal-directed action and the formation of right and just relationships. These are the leaders who catalyze forces of human energy to be directed in service to the good that we share in common.

Spiritlinking leaders who illumine the way toward such transformative change manifest the cognitive resilience and character flexibility necessary to engage in consultation, consensus building, delegation and the effective management of differing positions. As these activities form the foundation for community building, these leaders invite their organizations to become part of the living covenant between human beings and the world matrix in which we live and work.

While their immediate sphere of influence is most assuredly within the institutions in which they work, spiritlinking leaders are cognizant of the seriousness of these times. Sensitive to the healing power of the metaphor, they are aware that their institutions, by their very integrity, serve to effect changes far beyond their own parameters. As a central paradigm for entering the next millennium with vibrancy and grace, they promote corporate interconnection as such networking emits energy and solidifies bonds across divergent populations. Such solidarity is transformative as interdependency sparks energy and insight, as light bends toward those parts of our world that suffer from escalating catastrophes of separatism and nationalism, of exploitation and domination.

To commit to working through resistance to transformative change within institutions is to take deliberate action toward bringing forth a more gracious planet. The global networking of organizational communities of differing disciplines and missions possesses a unique opportunity to serve as a value-based force for the common good. This cannot happen without the untiring efforts of leaders who sense that what they are about is far greater than the roles they fulfill in their particular institutions. Perhaps it is time for a long walk along desert paths with a motley assortment of unlikely companions. Perhaps it is time for those who are passionately committed to joining spirits and hearts to create a future where no refugee is without land, a future in which the mystery of the Earth and the stars relentlessly reminds us of our own life-stuff and beckons us to treat all creation with dignity and compassion. It is time to dare spiritlinking.

"It is time to dare spiritlinking."

You've Got the Last Word....

• A prominent church leader urges that at every meeting taking place in the diocese, the question be posed, "How does what we're doing have an impact on the poor?"[10] Similarly, spiritlinking leaders may ask their management teams, their employees, their boards of trustees, "How does our action harm or foster ecological healing?"

Consider the last three decisions your board made. Are there any potential effects on the environment? on the quality of life for your employees? for the surrounding community?

_____

_____

Identify five local leaders from spheres of influence different from your own. How might you engage them in conversation concerning the viability of your organizational mission and the potential you have to contribute to the common good?

_____

_____

How might you establish linkages with these persons? What might be gained from such networking?

_____

_____

What stops you, other than time, from making these connections?

_____

_____

Where will you go from here?

_____

_____

NOTES

1. M. Angelou, *Wouldn't Take Nothing for My Journey Now* (Toronto: Bantam Books, 1994), 33–34.

2. M. Wheatley, *Leadership and the New Science: Learning about Organization from an Orderly Universe* (San Francisco: Berrett-Koehler, 1994), 71.

3. A. MacLeish, quoted by J. Gleick in *Making a New Science* (New York: Penguin Books, 1988), 5.

4. For information concerning the Catholic Common Ground Initiative, contact the National Pastoral Life Center, New York, New York.

5. For an explication of this research, refer to: D. Nygren, M. Ukeritis, and D. McClelland, "Religious Leadership Competencies," *Review for Religious* (May-June 1993).

6. R. S. Jones, *Physics as Metaphor* (New York: Meridian, 1982), vii.

7. Nygren, Ukeritis and McClelland, 407.

8. D. Boadella, *Embyology and Therapy* (United Kingdom: Abbotsbury Publications, 1982), 101.

9. T. Berry, "Wonderworld as Wasteworld," *Cross Currents* 35 no. 4 (1985):5.

10. The Most Reverend Kenneth Untener, Bishop of Saginaw, Michigan.

RECOMMENDED READING

CHAPTER 1

Angelou, M. *Wouldn't Take Nothing for My Journey Now.* New York: Bantam Books, 1994.

Bennis, W., J. Parikh, and R. Lessem. *Beyond Leadership: Balancing Economics, Ethics and Ecology.* Cambridge, MA: Blackwell Publishers, 1994.

Wheatley, M. *Leadership and the New Science: Learning about Organization from an Orderly Universe.* San Francisco: Berrett-Koehler, 1994.

CHAPTER 2

Bennis, W. *Why Leader's Can't Lead: The Unconscious Conspiracy Continues.* San Francisco: Jossey-Bass, 1989.

Covin, T., and R. Kilmann. "Participant Perceptions of Positive and Negative Influences on Large-Scale Change." *Group and Organization Studies* 25, no. 2 (1990).

CHAPTER 3

Barker, J. *The Business of Discovering the Future.* San Francisco: Harper Business, 1993.

CHAPTERS 4 AND 5

Bandura, A. "Human Agency: The Emperor Does Have Clothes." Keynote Address, Proceedings of the Canadian Psychological Association Convention, June 1997.

Bellah, R., R. Madsen, W. Sullivan, A. Swidler, and S. Tipton. *The Good Society.* New York: Alfred A. Knopf, 1991.

Hodson, G., and R. M. Sorrentino. "Groupthink and Uncertainty Orientation: Personality Differences in Reactivity to Group Situation" in *Group Dynamics,* 1, no. 2 (1997).

Hollenbach, D. "The Catholic University and the Common Good" in *Current Issues in Higher Education,* 16, no. 1 (1995).

———. "The Common Good Revisited" in *Theological Studies, 50,* no. 1 (1989).

Janis, I. L. *Groupthink: Psychological Studies of Policy Decisions and Fiascoes.* Boston: Houghton Mifflin, 1982.

Lipman-Blumen, J. *The Connective Edge: Leading in an Interdependent World.* San Francisco: Jossey-Bass, 1996.

Markham, D. "Leadership: On Conflict, Groupthink and the Common Good" in *Origins,* November 13, 1997.

Nygren, D., M. Ukeritis, and D. McClelland. "Religious Leadership Competencies" in *Review for Religious* (May-June) 1993.

Rivers, F. *The Way of the Owl: Succeeding with Integrity in a Conflicted World.* San Francisco: Harper, 1996.

Roszak, T., M. E. Gomes, and A. D. Kanner, eds. *Ecopsychology: Restoring the Earth, Healing the Mind.* San Francisco: Sierra Club Books, 1995.

Tracy, D. *Plurality and Ambiguity: Hermeneutics, Religion, Hope.* San Francisco: Harper and Row, 1987.

Wren, J. T., ed. *The Leader's Companion: Insights on Leadership through the Ages.* New York: The Free Press, 1995.

CHAPTER 6

Conger, J. A. *The Charismatic Leader: Behind the Mystique of Exceptional Leadership.* San Francisco: Jossey-Bass, 1989.

Kets De Wries, M. *Leaders, Fools and Imposters: Essays on the Psychology of Leadership.* San Francisco: Jossey-Bass, 1993.

Martin, I. *From Couch to Corporation: Becoming a Successful Corporate Therapist.* Toronto: John Wiley & Sons, Inc., 1996.

CHAPTER 7

Berry, T. *The Dream of the Earth.* San Francisco: Sierra Club Books, 1990.

———. "Wonderworld as Wasteworld," *Cross Currents* 35, no. 4 (1985).

Boadella, D. *Embyology and Therapy.* United Kingdom: Abbotsbury Publications, 1982.

Capra, F., and D. Steindl-Rast. *Belonging to the Universe.* San Francisco: Harper, 1991.

Csikszentmihalyi, M. *Creativity: Flow and the Psychology of Discovery and Invention.* New York: HarperCollins, 1996.

Dufour, Y. "Grounding: An Exploration through Language and the Body." In *Manual for Training in Bioenergetic Analysis.* Toronto, 1997.

Lowen, A. *Depression and the Body.* New York: Coward, McCann & Geoghegan, 1972.

Whyte, D. *The Heart Aroused: Poetry and the Preservation of the Soul in Corporate America.* New York: Currency Doubleday, 1994.

Advance Praise for *Spiritlinking Leadership*

"Dr. Markham not only brings light to the core of being a leader today, but follows each concept with practical questions to be used as tools for board meetings, planning sessions, retreats and team meetings. This is a 'working' book that will become a tool to be used on a routine basis."

—William F. Loving
CEO, ScanCAD International, Inc.

"This is a challenging and courageous book that anyone who is in a position of leadership should read. Donna Markham looks with unblinking honesty and gentle humor at all the difficulties that any organization may face: conflict, resistance to change, the denial of the truth of what is happening, our own fears and self-deceptions. She invites us to see how we can meet these challenges without fear and find a way through to new life, community and creativity. She offers a wonderful and positive vision of leadership, with practical advice on what to do. She is unerringly accurate in showing up all the ways in which we may evade the challenges of good leadership, but offers hope and practical advice. And she has wonderful stories to tell."

—Father Timothy Radcliffe, O.P.
Master of the Dominican Order

"Dr. Donna Markham has written a book that is essential for leaders as we move into the new millennium. *Spiritlinking Leadership* adds a fresh, new dimension to organizational dynamics. It can aid leaders in creating, reorganizing and transforming their organizations to meet the ever increasing demand for organizational environments to support and welcome diversity. It not only answers the question, 'Can we create a world that works for everyone?' It shows us how to create such a world."

—Aeeshah Ababio Clottey
Executive Director, Center for Racial Healing

"We live in a time of global mercantile communities, where interconnection is immediate and competition profound. We correctly acknowledge that professional passions and competitive fears require constant attention through the medium of choice, and that mentoring and motivation are prerequisite for success. Donna Markham has found a path to link the esoteric awareness of spirit with the exoteric necessities of commerce, leadership and the inevitability of constant change. The result is a way out of chaos. *Spiritlinking Leadership* is a must read. I hope you join me in its truth."

—Rolland G. Smith
Journalist

"*Spiritlinking Leadership* provides valuable insights and practical strategies for today's health care executives who are called upon to transform their organizations in the midst of chaos. Dr. Markham shows us how to harness the energy of the spirit to effectively manage conflict and resistance to change. Must reading for all leaders dedicated to building healthier communities and a more just society."

—Richard J. Kramer
President/CEO, Catholic Healthcare West

"Donna Markham's *Spiritlinking Leadership* provides creative insights that can help guide organization leaders and others into the twenty-first century. Her innovative approach captures the essence of the human spirit and how to integrate it effectively into contemporary organizational cultures. In the ever increasing competitive challenges of today's global marketplace, *Spiritlinking Leadership* provides a thoughtful and pragmatic road map to business organizational development strategies—ones that can be filled with a vibrant sense of fun, sensitive humane relationships and financial success."

—Jay D. Hair, Ph.D.
President Emeritus, National Wildlife Federation (USA)

"Dr. Donna Markham skillfully speaks of the oneness, the connectedness of all things. She gives us definite steps that describe how this understanding, when implemented by those in leadership roles, can benefit businesses and nonprofits."

—Dennis Weaver
Actor and Environmentalist

"Dr. Markham has given leaders of mission-driven, value-based organizations an excellent template for managing change. This book provides leadership guidelines that can assist management in getting the most from the resources entrusted to their care."

—Oliver W. Wesson, Jr.
Former President, J. P. Morgan Community Development Corporation

"Leaders, regardless of their specific religions, homelands or organizations to which they are affiliated, and which they lead, find themselves getting lost more and more in the 'black hole' of materialism, competition, individualism and loneliness. The new concept of 'spiritlinking leadership' that Donna J. Markham is imprinting in the area of leadership service is a promising and refreshing one, which focuses on empowering the linkage between leaders by means of spirituality, sharing, social commitment and justice, providing a new option for leaders in the coming millennium. The personal examples, metaphors and insights are impressive in vividly portraying Dr. Markham's message to form an ecological, healing network of leaders who aim to foster global, social and individual well-being."

—Dina Feldman
Director of the Division of Research, Evaluation and Planning
Mental Health Services Department, Ministry of Health, Jerusalem, Israel